5 Ingredients or Less
Crock Pot Express Cookbook

Top 100 Tasty and Healthy Recipes for Your Crock Pot Express Multi-cooker

By
Pamela Harmon

Copyright©2019 by Pamela Harmon

All rights reserved.

Legal Notice:

The book is copyright protected. This is only for personal use. You cannot amend, distribute, sell, use, quote or paraphrase any part or the content within this book without the consent of the author.

Disclaimer Notice:

Please note the information contained within this document is for educational and entertainment purposes only. Every attempt has been made to provide accurate, up to date and reliable complete information. No warranties of any kind are expressed or implied. Readers acknowledge that the author is not engaging in the rendering of legal, financial, medical or professional advice. The content of this book has been derived from various sources. Please consult a licensed professional before attempting any techniques outlined in this book.

By reading this document, the reader agrees that under no circumstances are is the author responsible for any loses, direct or indirect, which are incurred as a result the use of information contained within this document, including, but not limited to, —errors, omissions, or inaccuracies.

Table of Contents

Introduction 1

Chapter 1 What is the CrockPot Express? 2

    The Crock-Pot Express Buttons 2

    How to Use the Crock-Pot Express 4

    Changing the Settings While Cooking 4

    Tips on Using the Crock-Pot Express 6

Chapter 2: Steamed Recipes 8

    Easy and Healthy Steamed Asparagus 8

    Chili-Ginger Steamed Chicken 9

    CrockPot Express Steamed Cauliflower 10

    New Orleans' Style Shrimps 11

    Steamed Garlic and Parsley Mussels 12

    Scallion-Ginger Steamed Cod 13

    Steamed Lemon-Garlic Broccoli 14

    Very Easy Steamed Artichokes 15

    Steamed Fish Tuscan Style 16

    Steamed and Herbed Halibut 17

Chapter 3: Soup Recipes 18

    Chicken Dumpling Soup 18

    Easy Tomato Soup 19

    Cheesy Broccoli Soup 20

    Minty Pea Soup 21

    Spicy and Cheesy Corn Soup 22

    Leeks and Bacon on Potato Chowder 23

    Easy-Peasy Clam Chowder 24

Cauliflower Soup with Coco-Curry 25
Chicken in Green Enchilada Soup 26
Chorizo and Kale Soup 27
Primavera Soup with Tortellini 28
Mushroom and Wild Rice Soup 29
Barley and Beef Soup 30
White Bean and Chicken Soup Southwest Style 31
Chicken Pesto Soup 32

Chapter 4: Poultry Recipes 33

Pan Fried Chicken Salsa 33
Stewed Pineapple Chicken 34
Pan Fried Chicken with Spinach Artichoke Sauce 35
Bacon and Tomato Chicken 36
Pan Fried Chicken Thighs with Balsamic-Cranberry Reduction 37
Asparagus and Lemon Chicken 38
Garlic and Lemon Slow Cooked Chicken 39
Slow Cooked Salsa Verde Chicken 40
Shredded Chicken BBQ 41
Delicious Teriyaki Chicken 42
Shepherd's Pie Style Turkey 43
Slow-Cooked Chicken in Hoisin Sauce 44
Easy and Delish Chicken Curry 45
Tomato-Balsamic Chicken 46
Stir Fried Chicken Caribbean Style 47

Chapter5: Beans/Chili Recipes 48

Shrimp and Black Bean Enchiladas 48
Sweet Potato and Black Bean Chili 49

White Beans and Sausages 50

Easy White Chicken Chili 51

Simple 5-Ingredient Chili 52

Slow Cooker Chickpea and Sweet Potato Stew 53

Chickpea Tomato Soup with Rosemary 54

Crock-Pot Chicken Enchilada Soup 55

Bean Turkey Chili 56

Beefy Corn and Black Bean Chili 57

Sausage and Bean Jambalaya 58

Cowboy Beef 59

Overnight Chili 60

5-Ingredient Black Bean Soup 61

Slow Cooked Mexican Meatball Stew 62

Chapter 6: Meat/Stew Recipes 63

Slow Cooked Baby Back Ribs 63

Thai Coconut Pork Curry 64

Mushroom Pork Chops 65

Peach Pork Picante 66

Quick Swedish Meatballs 67

Orange Beef 68

Pulled Pork 69

Slow Cooked Cranberry Pork Chop 70

Easy Slow Cooked Ham 71

Slow Cooked Mississippi Roast 72

Slow Cooked Honey Mustard Barbecue Pork Ribs 73

Slow Cooked Corned Beef and Cabbages 74

Slow Cooked Ancho Beef Stew 75

5- Ingredient Stew 76

Slow Cooked Beef Pot Roast 77

Chapter 7: Rice/Risotto Recipes 78

Simple Mexican Quinoa 78

Easy Vegetable Fried Rice 79

Rice with Parsley, Almonds, And Apricots 80

Mexican Brown Rice 81

5- Ingredient Fried Rice 82

One-Pot Fried Rice 83

5-Ingredient Risotto 84

Easy Risotto with Bacon 85

Mushroom, Leek, And Brie Risotto 86

Chicken Fried Rice 87

Chapter 8: Dessert Recipes 88

Slow Cooked 3-Ingredient Peach Cobbler 88

Slow Cooker Fudge 89

Crockpot Monkey Bread 90

Slow Cooked Lemon Blueberry Dump Cake 91

Crock-Pot Express Chocolate Bars 92

Chapter 9: Slow Cooker Recipes 93

Slow and Easy Beef Stew 93

Italian Turkey Crock-Pot Express Soup 94

Crock-Pot Express Spicy Honey Garlic BBQ Meatballs 95

One-Pot Tortellini Alfredo 96

Vegetable Frittata 97

Crock-Pot Express Chicken Curry 98

Easy Sweet and Sour Chicken 99

Crock-Pot Express Peach Salsa Chicken 100

Chicken Broccoli Alfredo 101

Cranberry Chicken Legs 102

Breakfast Casserole in Crock-Pot Express 103

Egg, Spinach, and Ham Breakfast Casserole 104

Egg, Bacon, And Hash Brown Casserole 105

Slow Cooked Chicken and Gravy 106

Crock-Pot Express Creamy Taco Chicken 107

Introduction

There are so many benefits of preparing your own meals at home. First, cooking our own meals can save you a lot of money than when you go and eat at a restaurant. Another reason why you should cook your own food is that you know what goes into your food thus you have the choice of what goes into your food and what doesn't. In fact, cooking your own meals at home is deemed healthier than eating out.

But even if it is genuinely ideal to cook your own meals at home, there are moments when you just do not have enough time as well as ingredients to make delicious foods at home. Would it be nice if you can cook delicious meals without using too many ingredients and spending too much time in the kitchen? This is when this book comes in handy.

This eBook is dedicated to educating you how to cook delicious meals using the newest kitchen innovation—Crock-Pot Express. We understand that it is difficult for most people to eat home-cooked meals because they are always on to go. Moreover, whipping up foods that are made from 10 or more ingredients is challenging because not everyone has all the ingredients in their pantry. This is the reason why we omit in our recipes salt, pepper, and water as we know that these are the only kitchen staples most people have.

The aim of this book is to make cooking simple, fun, and practical. Thus, this book is not only perfect for busy people who loved to cook yet don't have enough time but even for singles that do not have exceptional kitchen skills. With this book, you don't have to jump from one store to the other to find the ingredients needed to create delicious meals. You can even scavenge with whatever it is you have available in your pantry.
Enjoy!

Chapter 1 What is the Crock Pot Express?

The Crock-Pot Express is one of the newest kitchen devices that you can use to make cooking easier and fun. It is a top-of-the-line electric pressure cooker that also functions as a slow cooker. And compared to its contemporaries, it is also very affordable thus giving you a bang for your buck.

The Crock-Pot Express Buttons

Just like other electric pressure cookers, the Crock-Pot Express also comes with pre-set cooking buttons that allow you to cook different meals like a pro. There are nine (9) pre-set cooking buttons in the Crock-Pot Express and it is important to get to know what these buttons are and their pre-set cooking time. Take note that all pre-set buttons cook under high pressure unless indicated.

- **Steam:** This button allows you to steam for 10 minutes. But you can adjust the cooking time from 3 minutes to 1 hour. You can adjust the cooking time by pressing the "+" or "-" button. This works for all types of pre-set cooking buttons. 3 minutes is the shortest cooking time available for the Crock-Pot Express but if you want to cook something less than that, set a timer and press the "Stop" button after the timer has set off.
- **Poultry:** Cook chicken, turkey, and other game fowl dishes within 15 minutes. You can adjust the cooking time from 15 minutes to 2 hours.
- **Soup:** You can cook soup using the pre-set cooking time of 30 minutes, but you can adjust the cooking time from 5 minutes to 2 hours.
- **Beans/Chili:** Cook chili, beans, or stew in 20 minutes. You can adjust the cooking time from 5 minutes to 2 hours.
- **Meat/Stew:** Cook all types of meat from beef, lamb, pork, and many others using the pre-set cooking time of 35 minutes. You can adjust the cooking time from 15 minutes to 2 hours.

- **Rice/Risotto:** Cook rice dishes and risotto within 12 minutes at low pressure. The range of cooking time can be adjusted from 6 minutes to 30 minutes.
- **Multigrain:** Multigrain foods such as pasta, quinoa, and barley to name a few can be cooked in 40 minutes as the pre-set cooking time. You can adjust the cooking time from 10 minutes to 2 hours.
- **Dessert:** Cook all types of desserts at low pressure for 10 minutes. You can adjust the cooking time from 5 minutes to 2 hours.
- **Yogurt:** This button is not a pressure cooker function. It uses low temperature necessary for good bacteria to flourish for fermentation. It works for 8 hours but can be adjusted from 6 hours to 12 hours.
- **Slow Cook:** This is not a pressure cooker function, but it cooks food at high temperature at the pre-set cooking time of 4 hours. The cooking time can be adjusted from 30 minutes to 20 hours. You can adjust the cooking temperature from low to high, yet we recommend the low temperature setting for best results.
- **Brown/Sauté:** This is also not a pressure cooker function and it requires you to open the lid when using this function. It cooks food at high temperature for 30 minutes, but you can adjust the cooking time to 5 minutes at the minimum. The temperature setting can also be adjusted from low to high.
- **Keep Warm:** Also not a pressure cooker function, this button allows you to warm your food for 4 hours so that you can keep your food warm by the time you are ready to eat. You can set the warmer function to 30 minutes at the minimum.
- **Delay timer:** This button allows you to cook food at a later time.

It is important to take note that the Crock-Pot Express does not know what you put into your pot thus the pre-set cooking button is merely suggested times for cooking your food. This means that you are free to choose which type of button you want regardless of what food you cook. For instance, you can cook chicken soup using the Meat/Stew button and it will still work out fine. The thing is that choose the closest cooking time to the pre-set button that you know that will cook your food. This is the reason why it is so important to know about the pre-set buttons and their range.

How to Use the Crock-Pot Express

The Crock-Pot Express has four major components, and these include the lid, steaming rack, inner cooking pot, and the electronic housing with the heating base. When using the pot, make sure that the inner pot is placed into the heating base. The lid can be closed such that the inverted triangle is aligned to the image of a closed lock. To cook your favorite food, below are the steps on how to use the Crock-Pot Express:

- Add all ingredients into the inner cooking pot.
- Close and secure the lid. For most functions, make sure that the Steam Release Valve is set to sealed. Other functions such as Slow Cook and Yogurt require the Steam Release Valve to be on release mode. The Brown/Sauté function does not need the lid to be placed on while cooking.
- Press the button that you want to use and adjust the temperature or pressure if necessary. There are separate buttons on the Control Panel for the pressure and temperature with the corresponding "low" or "high" options.
- Use the Time Selection button to choose the cooking time. This feature is necessary especially if you are not using the pre-set cooking time. Just press any of the "+" or "-" buttons just below the small digital screen.
- Press the Start/Stop button to turn on the Crock-Pot Express.
- Once the cooking is complete, wait for at least 10 minutes to allow the pressure to release naturally. If not, use a long kitchen utensil to rotate the Steam Release Valve to the "release" position.

Changing the Settings While Cooking

Using the Crock-Pot Express is very easy but what if you are in the middle of cooking and you realize that your settings are all wrong? Not to worry, switching to different functions and settings while cooking is not difficult. Below are the steps on how you can operate your Crock-Pot Express.

Switching Functions:

- Press the Start/Stop button and press the new cooking function.
- A new timer will flash on the electronic screen including the selected function.
- Choose the desired time, temperature, and pressure.
- Press the Start/Stop button so that the new function can start cooking your food.

Change Cooking Time

- To change the cooking time before cooking starts, press the "+" or "-" buttons.
- Press and release to change the cooking time slowly until you achieve the desired cooking time.
- Once you achieve the desired cooking time, press the Start/Stop button.
- If you have already started cooking yet you want to adjust, press the Start/Stop button and do the first step over.

Change Pressure and Temperature

You can easily change the pressure of a particular pre-set function or button before the cooking starts. Press the Pressure Adjust button to "high" or "low" before pressing the Start/Stop button. The same thing can be done to change the temperature. Look for the Temp Adjust button before pressing the Start/Stop button.

Remember that if the Crock-Pot Express is running and you want to change the setting, always press the Start/Stop button to cancel out the cooking process before making any changes on the setting.

Tips on Using the Crock-Pot Express

Using the Crock-Pot Express is no rocket science. It is a straight-forward kitchen appliance with a very simple control panel thus using it is very easy even for first timers. But for you to be able to enjoy using this intuitive kitchen helper, below are great tips that you can follow:

- **Always cook in the inner pot:** Never forget to place the inner pot inside the Crock-Pot Express. Never add ingredients inside the pressure cooker housing without the inner pot because it contains all the electrical components in it. You might get electrocuted. Moreover, when putting the inner pot inside, make sure that it is dry.
- **Always use enough liquid:** It is recommended that you use at least 1 cup of water or liquid to cook your food so that it can generate enough heat and pressure to cook your food.
- **Do not fill the cooking pot with too much ingredients:** The inner cooking pot comes with a MAX line that indicates that you should never put food past the line otherwise, it will not cook your food properly as there is not enough space for the gas and heat to expand inside the pressure cooker.
- **Use the appropriate accessories:** When you buy the Crock-Pot Express, it comes with its own steaming rack and ladle. Make sure that you use them and no other accessories as they are designed not to damage the surface of the inner cooking pot.
- **Remove the lid carefully:** Opening the lid of a hot Crock-Pot Express can be dangerous. The steam that comes out from the pressure cooker once you open the lid can be scalding hot. Use a lid handle and make sure that you open the lid away from you so that the steam can escape safely.
- **Do not use the cooking pot on stovetop:** Remember that the inner cooking pot is designed to be used only for the Crock-Pot Express. Never use it on stove top, in the oven, or microwave otherwise it will damage the pot.
- **Always clean the Crock-Pot Express after every use:** It is critical to clean the Crock-Pot Express after every use. For the electric housing, wipe the surface with dry cloth.

Pay extra attention to the lid and make sure that the Steam Release Valve is free from any trapper dirt as well as wear and tear on the O-ring.

- **Do not force the lid to open:** If you are trying to open the Crock-Pot Express and the lid does not open easily, then don't force it. This means that the multi-cooker is still under pressure. Leave it for 10 minutes and you should be able to open it without any problems.

Chapter 2: Steamed Recipes

Easy and Healthy Steamed Asparagus

Serves: 2

Cooking Time: 1 minute

Ingredients
- 1 lemon, cut into wedges
- Pepper and salt to taste
- 1 tbsp extra virgin olive oil
- 1-lb medium asparagus stalks trimmed and peeled

Instructions
1. Add a cup of water in crock.
2. Place the steam rack and put asparagus on steam rack.
3. Cover, press steam button, and adjust for 3 minutes.
4. Do a quick release.
5. Immediately transfer steamed asparagus to a serving platter.
6. Drizzle with olive oil and lemon.
7. Season with pepper and salt.
8. Enjoy!

Nutrition information:

Calories per serving: 119; Carbohydrates: 12.6g; Protein: 5.52g; Fat: 7.12g; Fiber: 5.2g

Chili-Ginger Steamed Chicken

Serves: 5

Cooking Time: 45 minutes

Ingredients

- 1 tbsp chopped cilantro
- 3-pcs fresh red chilies or to taste, chopped
- 3 tbsps sesame oil
- 3-inches fresh ginger, peeled and grated, divided
- 5-pieces skin on chicken thighs, soaked in water + 2 tbsps salt overnight

Instructions

1. Add a cup of water in crock.
2. In a heatproof a bowl that fits inside the crock, grease with sesame oil.
3. Discard soaking water, pat dry the chicken, place in a bowl, and swirl to cover with oil.
4. Season with ½ of ginger and the chilies to liking.
5. Cover, press steam button, and adjust the timer to 45 minutes.
6. Do a quick release.
7. Garnish chicken with remaining ginger and chopped cilantro. Toss well to coat.
8. Serve and enjoy.

Nutrition information:

Calories per serving: 415; Carbohydrates: 11.46g; Protein: 23.49g; Fat: 30.89g; Fiber: 2.3g

CrockPot Express Steamed Cauliflower

Serves: 2

Cooking Time: 15 minutes

Ingredients

- 2 tbsps salted butter
- 2 lemon wedges
- Salt to taste
- 1 large 2-lbs cauliflower, leaves still attached

Instructions

1. Add a cup of water in crock.
2. Place the washed cauliflower with leaves still attached to the steamer basket.
3. Salt the tops of the cauliflower.
4. Close lid, press steam button, and cook for 10 minutes.
5. In a small a bowl, melt butter and squeeze 1 lemon wedge.
6. Once cauliflower is done cooking, do a quick release.
7. Transfer to a bowl, drizzle with butter-lemon sauce.
8. Serve with a wedge of lemon and remaining sauce.

Nutrition information:

Calories per serving: 226; Carbohydrates: 25.86g; Protein: 9g; Fat: 12.9g; Fiber: 9.2g

New Orleans' Style Shrimps

Serves: 4

Cooking Time: 15 minutes

Ingredients

- 2-lbs shell on large shrimps, deveined
- 4 ears of corn, husked and halved
- 2 lemons, divided
- ¼ cup Zatarain's Crawfish, shrimp, & crab boil
- 2-lbs small red skinned potatoes

Instructions

1. Add 2 cups of water in crock.
2. Mix in Zatarain's.
3. Slice the lemons in half and squeeze a half of a lemon into to the pot. Slice the remaining lemons into wedges.
4. Clean and scrub the small potatoes and place in pot.
5. Place shrimps in a steamer basket and drizzle with the sauce from to the pot.
6. Top shrimps with the corn.
7. Cover, press steam button, and set time to 15 minutes.
8. When done cooking, do a quick release, and transfer corn, shrimps, and potatoes to a large a bowl.
9. Drizzle with sauce from pot. Season with salt if desired.
10. Serve with lemon wedges on the side.

Nutrition information:

Calories per serving: 454; Carbohydrates: 68.33g; Protein: 39.98g; Fat: 4.5g; Fiber: 8.3g

Steamed Garlic and Parsley Mussels

Serves: 4

Cooking Time: 15 minutes

Ingredients

- 2 tbsps olive oil
- 6 garlic cloves, chopped finely.
- ¼ cup fresh parsley, chopped finely
- 2-lbs mussels, scrubbed and rinsed
- 3 tbsps butter

Instructions

1. Press sauté button and choose high.
2. Once to the pot is hot, add oil and let it heat for a minute.
3. Stir in garlic and sauté until browned, around 3 minutes.
4. The add butter and melt for a minute. Turn pot off.
5. Place mussels in a heatproof a bowl that fits in to the pot. Pour the garlic-butter sauce on top of mussels and season with salt if desired.
6. Add a cup of water in crock, place steamer rack and place the a bowl of mussels on top.
7. Cover, press steam button, and steam for 10 minutes.
8. Do a quick release and remove a bowl of mussels.
9. Toss in parsley and serve.

Nutrition information:

Calories per serving: 339; Carbohydrates: 10.1g; Protein: 27.48g; Fat: 20.52g; Fiber: 0.2g

Scallion-Ginger Steamed Cod

Serves: 4

Cooking Time: 8 minutes

Ingredients

- 6 scallions, green parts cut into 3-inch lengths and white parts cut into ½-inch lengths
- 2 tbsps grated ginger
- 2 tbsps soy sauce
- 3 tbsps rice vinegar
- 4 6-oz skinless cod fillets
- Pepper and salt to taste

Instructions

1. In a heatproof bowl, mix well ginger, soy sauce, and vinegar.
2. Place cod fillets in the bowl and let soak in the sauce.
3. Season top of fillets with salt and pepper.
4. Top fillets with the chopped white onions.
5. Cover the dish with foil.
6. Add a cup of water in CrockPot Express, add the steamer rack, and place the dish of cod on top.
7. Cover, press steam button, and cook for 5 minutes.
8. Do a quick release, sprinkle green onions on top of fish.
9. Cover immediately and let it sit for 3 minutes.
10. Then remove the dish, serve, and enjoy.

Nutrition information:

Calories per serving: 139; Carbohydrates: 3.85g; Protein: 27.61g; Fat: 0.79g; Fiber: 0.9g

Steamed Lemon-Garlic Broccoli

Serves: 2

Cooking Time: 3 minutes

Ingredients
- 1 ½ tsps fresh lemon juice
- 1 ½ tbsps olive oil
- 1 garlic clove, peeled and minced
- 1 ¾-lb head of broccoli, cut into florets
- Salt and pepper to taste

Instructions
1. Press sauté button on CrockPot Express, choose high.
2. Once hot, add oil and let it heat for a minute.
3. Stir in garlic and sauté for 2 minutes or until lightly browned. Turn off.
4. In a heatproof dish that fits in the crock, place broccoli and season with pepper and salt.
5. In pot of garlic, stir in lemon juice and the drizzle on top of broccoli florets. Cover dish with foil.
6. Add a cup of water in crock, place the steamer rack, and put dish of broccoli on top.
7. Cover, press steam button, and steam for 3 minutes.
8. Do a quick release.
9. Serve and enjoy.

Nutrition information:

Calories per serving: 196; Carbohydrates: 16.42g; Protein: 13.25g; Fat: 12.23g; Fiber: 11.2g

Very Easy Steamed Artichokes

Serves: 4

Cooking Time: 35 minutes

Ingredients

- 1 lemon, halved
- ½ cup butter, melted
- Salt and pepper to taste
- 4 medium artichokes

Instructions

1. Clean artichokes by cutting off the top 1/3 and removing the outer leaves that are tough. Place in a steamer basket.
2. In Crock, place 2 cups of water and add the steamer basket.
3. Season artichokes generously with pepper and salt.
4. Cover, press steam button, and steam for 35 minutes.
5. Meanwhile, make the dip by mixing melted butter, ½ lemon, salt, and pepper. Mix well and adjust seasoning to taste. Keep warm.
6. Once artichokes are done cooking, do a quick release.
7. Transfer to a plate and serve with the lemon sauce.

Nutrition information:

Calories per serving: 287; Carbohydrates: 18.94g; Protein: 5.81g; Fat: 23.31g; Fiber: 9g

Steamed Fish Tuscan Style

Serves: 4

Cooking Time: 15 minutes

Ingredients

- Pepper and salt to taste
- 4 6-oz skinless cod fillet
- 1 14.5-oz can diced tomatoes with basil and oregano
- 1 large onion diced
- 1 tbsps olive oil

Instructions

1. In a heatproof dish that fits in your CrockPot express, grease sides with oil.
2. Spread diced onions on the bottom.
3. Place fillets on top of onion and season generously with pepper and salt.
4. Pour the can of diced tomatoes on top.
5. Cover dish securely with foil.
6. Add a cup of water in crock, place a steamer rack, and then add the dish.
7. Cover crock, press steam button, and steam for 10 minutes.
8. Do a natural release for 5 minutes and then do a quick release.
9. Serve and enjoy.

Nutrition information:

Calories per serving: 214; Carbohydrates: 14.22g; Protein: 27.45g; Fat: 4.68g; Fiber: g

Steamed and Herbed Halibut

Serves: 4

Cooking Time: 10 minutes

Ingredients

- 4 6-oz halibut fillets
- 1 tbsp dried dill weed
- 1 tsp garlic powder
- Pepper and salt to taste
- 1 lemon, divided
- 2 tsps dried parsley

Instructions

1. Ready a heatproof dish that fits in the crock.
2. Slice the lemon in half. Zest and juice ½ of the lemon and the other half, slice into thin circles.
3. Add the lemon slices on bottom of the dish and place halibut on top.
4. Season halibut with lemon juice, dill weed, garlic powder, pepper, and salt.
5. Cover dish securely with foil.
6. Add a cup of water in crock, place steamer rack and put the dish on top of rack.
7. Cover, press steam button, and steam for 10 minutes.
8. Do a quick release and garnish top with lemon zest.
9. Serve and enjoy.

Nutrition information:

Calories per serving: 329; Carbohydrates: 3.02g; Protein: 25.06g; Fat: 23.65g; Fiber: 0.4g

Chapter 3: Soup Recipes

Chicken Dumpling Soup

Serves: 6

Cooking Time: 15 minutes

Ingredients

- 2 10-oz cans chunk chicken, drained
- 2 14-oz cans chicken broth
- 2/3 cup milk
- 2 ¼ cups biscuit baking mix

Instructions

1. Mix well chicken broth and chunk chicken in CrockPot Express. Press sauté button and choose high. Bring to a constant simmer.
2. Meanwhile in a bowl, combine biscuit mix and milk until pulled together. Do not overmix. Separate the dough into 1-inch cubes and flatten.
3. Once the broth is simmering, drop the flattened dough into the broth until thoroughly covered.
4. Cover, press cancel, press soup button, and cook for 15 minutes.
5. Do a quick release, mix well, serve and enjoy.

Nutrition information:

Calories per serving: 361; Carbohydrates: 29.6g; Protein: 25g; Fat: 15.1g; Fiber: 0.8g

Easy Tomato Soup

Serves: 6

Cooking Time: 20 minutes

Ingredients

- Pepper and salt to taste
- 2 cups Progresso Chicken stock
- 2 28-oz cans whole plum tomatoes
- ¼ cup chopped fresh basil
- 3 cloves garlic, minced
- 1/3 cup heavy cream

Instructions

1. In a blender add the tomatoes and puree.
2. Add pureed tomatoes, chicken stock, garlic and half of the basil in CrockPot Express. Mix well.
3. Season with pepper and salt to taste.
4. Cover, press soup button, and cook for 20 minutes.
5. Do a quick release.
6. Mix well and adjust seasoning to taste.
7. Stir in heavy cream and serve.

Nutrition information:

Calories per serving: 76; Carbohydrates: 10.96g; Protein: 3.03g; Fat: 3.31g; Fiber: 5.2g

Cheesy Broccoli Soup

Serves: 6

Cooking Time: 20 minutes

Ingredients

- ½ small onion, diced
- 2 cups chopped broccoli florets
- 4 cups chicken stock
- 2 cups sharp cheddar cheese
- 15-oz can evaporated milk
- Pepper and salt to taste

Instructions

1. Add broccoli, onion, and chicken stock. Season generously with pepper and salt.
2. Cover, press soup button, and cook for 10 minutes.
3. Once done cooking, do a quick release. Press stop and press sauté function and choose high.
4. Transfer ½ of broccoli in a blender and ¼ cup of stock. Puree and return to the pot.
5. Stir in cheese. Cook and stir until melted, around 5 minutes.
6. Once the cheese is melted, stir in milk and adjust seasoning to taste.
7. Turn off the CrockPot, serve and enjoy.

Nutrition information:

Calories per serving: 278; Carbohydrates: 16.69g; Protein: 19.36g; Fat: 14.91g; Fiber: 0.2g

Minty Pea Soup

Serves: 4

Cooking Time: 25 minutes

Ingredients

- 1 tbsp fresh mint
- 3 ¼ cups vegetable stock
- 4 ½ cups frozen peas
- 1 white onion, chopped
- 1 baking potato, peeled and chopped
- Pepper and salt to taste

Instructions

1. Except for mint, add all ingredients in to the pot.
2. Cover, press soup button, and cook for 20 minutes.
3. Do a quick release. Press cancel, press sauté button, and choose high.
4. Season with pepper and salt.
5. With an immersion blender, blend soup along with mint.
6. Adjust seasoning if needed, serve, and enjoy.

Nutrition information:

Calories per serving: 225; Carbohydrates: 41.86g; Protein: 10.26g; Fat: 2.30g; Fiber: 9.32g

Spicy and Cheesy Corn Soup

Serves: 4

Cooking Time: 25 minutes

Ingredients

- ½ cup sharp cheddar cheese
- 1 large onion chopped
- 4 poblano chilies, seeded and chopped
- 2 cups fat-free milk, divided
- 1 16-oz package frozen corn, thawed, divided
- Pepper and salt to taste

Instructions

1. Add all ingredients in CrockPot Express except for milk and the cheese.
2. Season with pepper and salt. Mix well.
3. Cover, press soup button, and cook for 15 minutes.
4. Do a quick release. Press cancel, press sauté button, and choose high.
5. Stir in a cup of milk.
6. With an immersion blender, puree soup. If you want some chunks in your soup, set aside a cup or two of corn before pureeing.
7. Stir in cheese and cook for 8 minutes while stirring occasionally until melted and mixed well into the soup.
8. Stir in remaining milk and adjust seasoning if needed before serving.

Nutrition information:

Calories per serving: 260; Carbohydrates: 41.3g; Protein: 13.56g; Fat: 7.96g; Fiber: 9g

Leeks and Bacon on Potato Chowder

Serves: 4

Cooking Time: 30 minutes

Ingredients

- 1 12-oz can evaporated milk
- 1 ½-lbs Yukon gold potatoes, peeled and cubed
- 1 small onion, chopped
- ½-lb bacon strips, chopped
- 1 stalk green onions, chopped
- Pepper and salt to taste
- 1 ¼ cups water

Instructions

1. Press sauté ad choose high on your CrockPot Express.
2. Once hot, add Bacon and sauté until brown and crisped, around 7 minutes. Transfer browned bacon on a bowl and set aside.
3. Sauté onion in bacon grease for 5 minutes.
4. Stir in potatoes and water. Season generously with pepper and salt.
5. Cover, press soup button, and cook for 20 minutes.
6. Do a quick release. Press cancel, press sauté button and choose high.
7. Stir in milk.
8. With an immersion blender, puree soup.
9. Stir in green onions and bacon.
10. Adjust seasoning, serve, and enjoy.

Nutrition information:

Calories per serving: 271; Carbohydrates: 34g; Protein: 10g; Fat: 11g; Fiber: 2g

Easy-Peasy Clam Chowder

Serves: 5

Cooking Time: 20 minutes

Ingredients

- ¼ tsp ground nutmeg
- 2 6.5-oz cans chopped clams
- 1-2 cups cream
- 1 10.75-oz can condensed cream of potato soup, undiluted
- 1 10.75-oz can condensed cream of celery soup, undiluted
- Pepper and salt to taste

Instructions

1. In CrockPot Express, mix all ingredients except for cream.
2. Cover, press soup button, and cook for 15 minutes.
3. Do a quick release. Press cancel, press sauté button, and choose high.
4. Mix well and stir in a cup of cream.
5. Adjust seasoning to taste.
6. And if desired, you can add remaining cream.
7. Serve and enjoy.

Nutrition information:

Calories per serving: 251; Carbohydrates: 18g; Protein: 10g; Fat: 14g; Fiber: 3g

Cauliflower Soup with Coco-Curry

Serves: 4

Cooking Time: 25 minutes

Ingredients

- 1 cup coconut milk
- 1 32-oz carton vegetable broth
- 2 medium cauliflower heads, chopped into florets
- 3 tbsps yellow curry paste
- 1 tbsp grated ginger
- Pepper and salt to taste

Instructions

1. In CrockPot Express, mix vegetable broth, curry paste, and ginger. Mix well.
2. Add cauliflower florets and season with pepper.
3. Cover, press soup button, and cook for 15 minutes.
4. Do a quick release. Press cancel, press sauté button, and choose high.
5. Remove two ladle-full of cauliflower.
6. With an immersion blender, puree soup.
7. Return cauliflower and stir in coconut milk.
8. Cook for 5 minutes. Adjust seasoning if needed.
9. Serve and enjoy.

Nutrition information:

Calories per serving: 111; Carbohydrates: 10g; Protein: 3g; Fat: 8g; Fiber: 3g

Chicken in Green Enchilada Soup

Serves: 4

Cooking Time: 40 minutes

Ingredients

- 1 medium yellow onion, diced
- 1 4.5-oz can chopped green chiles
- 1 10-oz can Old El Paso green enchilada sauce
- 4 cups reduced sodium chicken broth
- 1 ½-lbs boneless, skinless chicken breasts, halved lengthwise
- Pepper and salt to taste

Instructions

1. In CrockPot Express, mix all ingredients.
2. Cover, press soup button, and cook for 40 minutes.
3. Do a quick release. Press cancel, press sauté button, and choose high.
4. Remove chicken breasts and shred with two forks. Return to the pot.
5. Adjust seasoning to taste.
6. Serve and enjoy.

Nutrition information:

Calories per serving: 335; Carbohydrates: 11.92g; Protein: 54.3g; Fat: 7.93g; Fiber: 1.8g

Chorizo and Kale Soup

Serves: 6

Cooking Time: 40 minutes

Ingredients

- 32-oz low sodium vegetable broth
- 1 14.5-oz can diced tomatoes
- 4 garlic cloves, minced
- 1 bunch kale, de-stemmed
- 1-lb chorizo, removed from casing
- Pepper and salt to taste

Instructions

1. Press sauté button and choose high.
2. Add chorizo in to the pot. Pound to separate while sautéing for 8 minutes or until browned.
3. Stir in garlic and continue cooking for 3 minutes.
4. Season with pepper and salt.
5. Stir in broth and tomatoes. Mix well.
6. Cover, press soup button, and cook for 10 minutes.
7. Meanwhile, tear kale leaf into bite-sized pieces.
8. Do a quick release.
9. Stir in kale, cover and let it sit for 10 minutes.
10. Adjust seasoning to taste, serve and enjoy.

Nutrition information:

Calories per serving: 443; Carbohydrates: 20.87g; Protein: 22.89g; Fat: 30.27g; Fiber: 5.5g

Primavera Soup with Tortellini

Serves: 4

Cooking Time: 15 minutes

Ingredients

- 2 tbsps thinly sliced fresh basil leaves
- 1 cup frozen peas
- 1 9-oz package cheese tortellini
- 1 10-oz package carrots, julienned
- 2 32-oz carton of reduced sodium chicken broth
- Pepper and salt to taste

Instructions

1. Press sauté button and choose high.
2. Bring broth to a boil.
3. Add tortellini. Bring to a boil.
4. Once boiling, cover, press cancel, press soup button, and cook for 10 minutes.
5. Do a quick release.
6. Stir in peas, basil leaves, and carrots. Adjust seasoning to taste.
7. After 5 minutes, serve, and enjoy.

Nutrition information:

Calories per serving: 282; Carbohydrates: 43g; Protein: 17g; Fat: 6g; Fiber: 5g

Mushroom and Wild Rice Soup

Serves: 8

Cooking Time: 30 minutes

Ingredients

- 2 cups heavy whipping cream
- 2 6-oz packages of long grain wild rice
- 1 tbsp chopped cilantro
- 1-lb baby Portobello mushrooms
- 1 32-oz carton reduced-sodium beef broth
- Pepper and salt to taste
- ½ cup water

Instructions

1. In CrockPot Express, mix well wild rice, mushrooms, broth, and water.
2. Season with pepper and salt, generously.
3. Cover, press soup button, and cook for 30 minutes.
4. Do a quick release.
5. Stir in whipping cream and cilantro. Mix well.
6. Adjust seasoning, if need.
7. Serve and enjoy.

Nutrition information:

Calories per serving: 375; Carbohydrates: 35g; Protein: 8g; Fat: 22g; Fiber: 2g

Barley and Beef Soup

Serves: 4

Cooking Time: 55 minutes

Ingredients

- 1 tsp ground mustard
- ¼ cup quick cooking barley
- 2 cups frozen mixed vegetables, thawed
- 3 cups beef broth
- 1-lb chuck steak, boneless
- Pepper and salt to taste

Instructions

1. Press sauté button and choose high.
2. Season chuck steak generously with pepper and salt.
3. A once to the pot is hot, add steak and brown each side for 5 minutes.
4. Transfer to cutting board, and chop into 1 to 2-inch pieces.
5. In pot, stir in barley and ground mustard. Sauté for 2 minutes.
6. Return chopped steak to the pot.
7. Add broth.
8. Cover, press soup button, and cook for 40 minutes.
9. Do a quick release.
10. Stir in thawed mixed vegetables. Cover and let it sit for another 5 minutes.
11. Adjust seasoning if needed before serving and enjoying.

Nutrition information:

Calories per serving: 340; Carbohydrates: 38.39g; Protein: 29.43g; Fat: 8.01g; Fiber: 6.4g

White Bean and Chicken Soup Southwest Style

Serves: 6

Cooking Time: 35 minutes

Ingredients

- 1 16-oz can cannellini beans, rinsed and drained
- 2 14-oz can chicken broth
- 1 tbsp taco seasoning
- 1-lb skinless, boneless chicken breast, sliced lengthwise
- ½ cup green salsa
- Pepper and salt to taste

Instructions

1. In CrockPot Express, mix well broth, seasoning, and salsa.
2. Add chicken and beans. Mix well.
3. Cover, press soup button, and cook for 30 minutes.
4. Do a quick release.
5. Remove chicken and shred with 2 forks.
6. Return shredded chicken to the pot and adjust seasoning if needed.
7. Serve and enjoy.

Nutrition information:

Calories per serving: 340; Carbohydrates: 6.26g; Protein: 47.21g; Fat: 12.9g; Fiber: 2.1g

Chicken Pesto Soup

Serves: 6

Cooking Time: 35 minutes

Ingredients

- 1/3 cup pesto
- 2 14-oz can cannellini beans
- 1-lb skinless, boneless chicken breasts, cut in half, lengthwise
- 3 cups fresh spinach
- 4 cups chicken stock
- Pepper and salt to taste

Instructions

1. In CrockPot Express, mix well pesto and chicken stock.
2. Add beans and chicken. Season with pepper and salt.
3. Cover, press soup button, and cook for 30 minutes.
4. Do a quick release.
5. Remove chicken and stir in spinach.
6. While shredding chicken with two forks and then return to the pot.
7. Stir well and adjust seasoning if needed.
8. Serve and enjoy.

Nutrition information:

Calories per serving: 257; Carbohydrates: 13.16g; Protein: 24.43g; Fat: 12.07g; Fiber: 3.1g

Chapter 4: Poultry Recipes

Pan Fried Chicken Salsa

Serves: 4
Cooking Time: 30 minutes

Ingredients

- 2 tbsps sour cream
- 1 cup cheddar cheese, shredded
- 1 cup salsa
- 4 tsps taco seasoning mix
- 4 skinless, boneless chicken breast halves, sliced in half

Instructions

1. Press sauté button and choose high.
2. In a heatproof baking dish that fits inside the CrockPot Express, place chicken.
3. Add taco seasoning and rub all over the chicken.
4. Pan fry chicken in batches for 3 minutes per side. Return browned chicken to the baking dish when done pan frying.
5. Cover chicken with salsa and then top with cheese.
6. Cover dish with securely with foil.
7. Add a cup of water in crock, place a steamer rack, and put dish on top.
8. Cover, press steam button, and steam for 15 minutes.
9. For 10 minutes, allow a natural release.
10. Then do a quick release.
11. Serve chicken with sour cream and enjoy.

Nutrition information:

Calories per serving: 287; Carbohydrates: 6.8g; Protein: 35.5g; Fat: 12.4g; Fiber: 1g

Stewed Pineapple Chicken

Serves: 5

Cooking Time: 40 minutes

Ingredients

- 1 tbsp oil
- 1 large orange, sliced into rounds
- 1 15-oz can pineapple chunks
- 1 ½ 1-oz packages dry onion soup mix
- Pepper and salt to taste
- 1 ¼ cups water
- 5 skinless, boneless chicken breasts, sliced in half, lengthwise

Instructions

1. Press sauté button and choose high.
2. Season chicken with pepper and salt.
3. Add oil to the pot and let it heat for 2 minutes.
4. Add chicken and brown for 4 minutes per side, in batches if needed.
5. Meanwhile in a large a bowl, pour in pineapple juice. Mix in onion soup mix and mix well.
6. Once the chicken is done browning, transfer to a plate.
7. Pour in water and deglaze to the pot. Stir in pineapple juice mixture and mix well.
8. Add back the chicken. And add ½ of the pineapple chunks.
9. Cover, press cancel, press stew button, and cook for 20 minutes.
10. Do a quick release.
11. Stir in remaining pineapples and orange slices. Mix well.
12. Serve and enjoy.

Nutrition information:

Calories per serving: 245; Carbohydrates: 22.8g; Protein: 25.8g; Fat: 5.8g; Fiber: 2.1g

Pan Fried Chicken with Spinach Artichoke Sauce

Serves: 4

Cooking Time: 35 minutes

Ingredients

- 2 tbsps oil
- 2 14-oz jars roasted garlic Alfredo pasta sauce
- 1 10-oz box frozen, chopped spinach, thawed and squeezed of excess liquid
- 4 boneless, skinless chicken breasts, halved lengthwise
- 1 14-oz jar marinated artichoke hearts, chopped
- Pepper and salt to taste

Instructions

1. Press sauté button and choose high.
2. Season chicken with pepper and salt.
3. Add oil to to the pot and let it heat for a minute then add chicken breasts. Brown and cook for 6 minutes per side and if needed brown in batches. Transfer to a plate after cooking and set aside. Chicken juices should be clear to not that is thoroughly cooked.
4. In the same pot, add chopped artichoke hearts and spinach. Stir-fry for 3 minutes, while deglazing pot.
5. Stir in Alfredo sauce and cook for 5 minutes or until heated through.
6. Return chicken to the pot or serve sauce over chicken.

Nutrition information:

Calories per serving: 445; Carbohydrates: 34.32g; Protein: 48.36g; Fat: 9.07g; Fiber: 12.1g

Bacon and Tomato Chicken

Serves: 3

Cooking Time: 25 minutes

Ingredients

- 1 tsp chopped cilantro
- ¼ cup diced bacon
- 2 Roma tomatoes, chopped
- 2 8-oz boneless, skinless chicken breasts, halved lengthwise
- 1 small onion, chopped
- Pepper and salt to taste
- ¼ cup water

Instructions

1. Press sauté button and choose high.
2. Season chicken with salt and pepper.
3. Add bacon to the pot and cook for 5 minutes or until brown and toasty. Transfer to a bowl.
4. Add chicken and fry in bacon grease for 5 minutes per side. Transfer to a plate after browning.
5. Add onions and sauté for 3 minutes until softened.
6. Add tomatoes and sauté until wilted and curled, around 4 minutes.
7. Add water and deglaze to the pot.
8. Add chicken, mix well, and simmer for 5 minutes.
9. Stir in cilantro, garnish with bacon, serve, and enjoy.

Nutrition information:

Calories per serving: 337; Carbohydrates: 40.16g; Protein: 17.24g; Fat: 12.57g; Fiber: 4.2g

Pan Fried Chicken Thighs with Balsamic-Cranberry Reduction

Serves: 4
Cooking Time: 40 minutes

Ingredients

- 4 chicken thighs, with skin and bone
- 1 tsp fresh thyme
- ¼ cup balsamic vinegar
- 1 ½ cups cranberries
- 2 tbsps honey
- Pepper and salt to taste

Instructions

1. Press sauté button and choose high.
2. Season chicken with pepper and salt, generously.
3. Pan fry chicken with skin side down for 10 minutes. Reduce heat to low and turnover chicken, pan fry for 10 minutes more. Remove chicken skin and discard. Turnover chicken once again and fry the other side without skin for 5 minutes. Transfer to a plate.
4. Return heat to high.
5. In the same pot, add cranberries, vinegar, honey, and thyme.
6. Deglaze the pot and mix well.
7. Return chicken to the pot and continue to simmer for 10 minutes, until sauce is reduced.
8. Serve and enjoy.

Nutrition information:
Calories per serving: 317; Carbohydrates: 16g; Protein: 23g; Fat: 18g; Fiber: 1g

Asparagus and Lemon Chicken

Serves: 4

Cooking Time: 25 minutes

Ingredients

- 2 lemons, sliced into rounds
- 2 cups chopped asparagus
- 4 tbsps butter, divided
- 2 pcs skinless, boneless chicken breast, cut into 4x1-inch lengths
- 2 tsps dried thyme, divided
- Pepper and salt to taste

Instructions

1. Press sauté button and choose high.
2. Season chicken with salt and pepper.
3. Add butter, 1 tsp thyme, and chicken. Stir-fry for 15 minutes until browned. Transfer to a plate.
4. Add 1 tbsp butter to to the pot and sauté asparagus and half of the lemons. Season with pepper and salt. Sauté for 5 minutes until asparagus is nearly tender.
5. Return chicken. Sauté for 3 minutes more.
6. Toss in remaining thyme, butter, and lemon. Sauté for a minute
7. Serve and enjoy.

Nutrition information:

Calories per serving: 254; Carbohydrates: 16.1g; Protein: 27.4g; Fat: 9g; Fiber: 5g

Garlic and Lemon Slow Cooked Chicken

Serves: 8

Cooking Time: 4 hours

Ingredients

- Pepper and salt to taste
- 5 sprigs fresh Rosemary
- 1 4-lb whole chicken
- 3 heads of garlic
- 4 lemons

Instructions

1. Grease CrockPot Express with cooking spray.
2. Cut garlic heads in half and lay on bottom of pot in a single layer, reserve half a garlic head.
3. Cut 3 lemons into 4 equal rounds and place on top of garlic. Cut remaining lemon into wedges and set aside.
4. Season chicken generously with pepper and salt, including the cavity of the chicken. Place a rosemary sprig in cavity as well as remaining garlic head and quartered lemon.
5. Place the chicken on top of the bed of lemons and garlic.
6. Cover, press slow cook button, and cook for 4 hours on high, or more.
7. To check if the chicken is cooked, the internal temperature should be 165°F.
8. Remember: not to open pot while cooking.
9. Serve and enjoy when done.

Nutrition information:

Calories per serving: 522.75; Carbohydrates: 3.65g; Protein: 54.8g; Fat: 30.86g; Fiber: 1.12g

Slow Cooked Salsa Verde Chicken

Serves: 6

Cooking Time: 3 to 5 hours

Ingredients

- 1/3 cup cilantro, chopped
- 1 ½ cups Monterey Jack cheese, shredded
- 1 16-oz jar salsa verde
- 4 boneless skinless chicken breasts, cut in half lengthwise
- Pepper and salt to taste

Instructions

1. Press sauté button on CrockPot Express and choose high.
2. Season chicken generously with pepper and salt.
3. Brown sides of chicken for 4 minutes per side.
4. Press stop button, press slow cook button, and choose low.
5. Evenly spread salsa verde over chicken.
6. Evenly top with cilantro and then followed by cheese.
7. Cover and cook on low for 5 hours or on high for 3 hours.

Nutrition information:

Calories per serving: 343.33; Carbohydrates: 5.77g; Protein: 45.81g; Fat: 15.38g; Fiber: 1.6g

Shredded Chicken BBQ

Serves: 12
Cooking Time: 7 hours

Ingredients

- 6 Hamburger buns
- 1 14-oz bottle of barbecue sauce
- ¼ cup light brown sugar
- 1 cup water
- 3-lbs chicken breasts, cut in half lengthwise
- Pepper and salt to taste

Instructions

1. Press sauté button and choose high.
2. Season chicken with pepper and salt, generously.
3. Pan fry chicken for 5 minutes per side.
4. Meanwhile, in a bowl mix barbecue sauce, brown sugar, and water.
5. Press stop button, click on slow cook function, and choose high.
6. Pour barbecue sauce mixture over chicken.
7. Cover and cook for 6 hours.
8. Once done, remove chicken, shred with two forks.
9. Return chicken and mix well.
10. Serve with toasted hamburger buns and enjoy.

Nutrition information:

Calories per serving: 380; Carbohydrates: 35.46g; Protein: 42.58g; Fat: 6.16g; Fiber: 1.7g

Delicious Teriyaki Chicken

Serves: 6
Cooking Time: 5 hours

Ingredients

- 1 stalk green onions, chopped
- 2-lbs chicken breasts, halved lengthwise
- ¼ cup chicken broth
- 1 tbsp honey
- 2/3 cup Teriyaki sauce
- Pepper and salt to taste

Instructions

1. Press sauté button and choose high.
2. Season chicken with pepper and salt.
3. Brown chicken for 4 minutes per side.
4. Meanwhile, mix well broth, teriyaki sauce, and honey.
5. Press stop button, then slow cook function, and choose low.
6. Pour teriyaki mixture over chicken. Cover and cook on low for 4 hours.
7. Remove chicken, shred with two forks, return to the pot, and mix well. Top with green onions and cook for another 30 minutes.
8. Serve and enjoy.

Nutrition information:

Calories per serving: 308; Carbohydrates: 8.87g; Protein: 51.15g; Fat: 6.12g; Fiber: 0.2g

Shepherd's Pie Style Turkey

Serves: 4

Cooking Time: 7 hours

Ingredients

- 1 20-oz package refrigerated mashed potatoes
- 1 tsp dried thyme, crushed
- 1 12-oz jar turkey gravy
- 1 10-oz package frozen mixed vegetables
- 12-oz turkey breast tenderloin, chopped into 1-inch cubes
- Pepper and salt to taste

Instructions

1. Evenly spread turkey on the bottom of Crock. Season with pepper, salt, and thyme.
2. Spread vegetable son top of turkey, followed by the gravy.
3. Drop the mashed potato in mounds covering the tops of the dish.
4. Cover, press slow cook button, and choose low.
5. Cook for 7 hours.
6. Serve and enjoy.

Nutrition information:

Calories per serving: 297; Carbohydrates: 33g; Protein: 27g; Fat: 5g; Fiber: 4g

Slow-Cooked Chicken in Hoisin Sauce

Serves: 6

Cooking Time: 3 hours

Ingredients

- 1 16-oz package frozen broccoli stir-fry blend, thawed
- ½ cup bottled hoisin sauce
- Pepper and salt to taste
- 2 tbsps quick cooking tapioca
- 12 chicken thighs, skin removed
- Cooking spray

Instructions

1. Lightly grease sides and bottom of CrockPot Express with cooking spray.
2. Place chicken. Season generously with pepper and salt. Sprinkle tapioca.
3. Spread hoisin sauce on top.
4. Cover, press slow cooker button and cook on high for 2 hours.
5. Add broccoli stir-fry blend on top, cover and continue cooking on high for another hour.
6. Before serving, mix well.

Nutrition information:

Calories per serving: 354; Carbohydrates: 37g; Protein: 32g; Fat: 6g; Fiber: 3g

Easy and Delish Chicken Curry

Serves: 6

Cooking Time: 4 hours

Ingredients

- 1 tbsp grated ginger
- 2 tsps curry powder
- 1 13.66-oz can of coconut milk
- 4 large chicken thighs, with bone and skin
- 1 16-oz package frozen stew vegetables
- Pepper and salt to taste
- ½ cup water

Instructions

1. Press sauté button and choose high.
2. Season chicken thighs with pepper and salt.
3. Place chicken, with skin side touching bottom of crockpot and brown for 7 minutes. Turn chicken over and brown the other side for 5 minutes, while discarding chicken skin. Once done browning, transfer chicken to a plate and set aside.
4. Add ginger to the pot and sauté for a minute.
5. Add curry powder and sauté for another minute.
6. Pour water and deglaze the pot.
7. Return chicken and arrange in an even layer in pot bottom.
8. Spread stew vegetables on top. And add ½ of coconut milk.
9. Cover, press stop, press slow cook function, and cook on high for 3 hours.
10. Stir in remaining coconut milk and continue cooking for another 30 minutes on low.
11. Adjust seasoning to taste before serving.

Nutrition information:

Calories per serving: 379; Carbohydrates: 12.97g; Protein: 23.14g; Fat: 27.27g; Fiber: 3.8g

Tomato-Balsamic Chicken

Serves: 6

Cooking Time: 5 hours

Ingredients

- 2.5-lbs boneless and skinless chicken thighs
- ¼ cup fresh basil leaves, chopped coarsely
- ½ cup grape tomatoes, quartered
- 1 tsp garlic, chopped
- 1 ¼ cups balsamic vinaigrette dressing

Instructions

1. Place chicken on bottom of the pot.
2. Add garlic and ½ cup of balsamic dressing.
3. Cover, press slow cook function and cook for 5 hours on low.
4. Transfer chicken to a serving plate.
5. Toss in quartered tomatoes and fresh basil leaves.
6. Drizzle with reserved balsamic dressing.
7. Serve and enjoy.

Nutrition information:

Calories per serving: 340; Carbohydrates: 4g; Protein: 39g; Fat: 18g; Fiber: 0g

Stir Fried Chicken Caribbean Style

Serves: 4

Cooking Time: 20 minutes

Ingredients

- 1 15-oz can mixed tropical fruit, drained and chopped coarsely
- 2 tsps Caribbean Jerk seasoning
- 1-lb boneless skinless chicken breasts, cut into ½-inch strips
- ¼ cup water
- 2 tsps cornstarch
- Pepper and salt to taste
- 2 8.8-oz packages of ready-to-serve brown rice

Instructions

1. Press sauté button and choose high.
2. Season chicken with pepper and salt.
3. Stir-fry chicken for 10 minutes, until no longer pink.
4. Add fruit and Jerk seasoning and sauté for a minute.
5. In a small a bowl, mix well water and cornstarch. Pour in the pot and continue mixing and cooking until thickened.
6. And then cook rice according to package instructions and serve chicken over rice.

Nutrition information:

Calories per serving: 265; Carbohydrates: 26.77g; Protein: 29.18g; Fat: 4.91g; Fiber: 2.5g

Chapter 5: Beans/Chili Recipes

Shrimp and Black Bean Enchiladas

Serves: 6
Cooking Time: 5 minutes

Ingredients

- 2 cans red or green enchilada sauce
- 2 cans black beans, drained and rinsed
- 1-pound shrimps, peeled and deveined
- 2 cups Mexican blend cheese, shredded
- 12 to 13 small tortillas

Instructions

1. Place the enchilada sauce, black beans, and shrimps in the Crock-Pot Express and give a good stir.
2. Pour in a cup of water and season with salt and pepper to taste.
3. Sprinkle with cheese on top.
4. Close the lid and make sure that the Steam Release Valve is in the sealed position.
1. Press the Start/Stop button first then the Beans/Chili button and adjust the cooking time to 5 minutes by pressing the "+" or "-" button.
5. Do natural pressure release.

Nutrition information:

Calories per serving: 622; Carbohydrates: 68.8g; Protein: 39.7g; Fat: 20.3g; Fiber: 8.5g

Sweet Potato and Black Bean Chili

Serves: 6
Cooking Time: 15 minutes

Ingredients

- 1 onion, diced
- 3 medium sweet potatoes, peeled and chopped
- 1 16-ounce jar salsa
- 1 15-ounce can black beans, drained and rinsed
- 2 tablespoon cumin powder

Instructions

1. Place all ingredients in the Crock-Pot Express.
2. Pour in 2 cups of water and season with salt and pepper to taste.
3. Give a good stir.
4. Close the lid and make sure that the Steam Release Valve is in the sealed position.
2. Press the Start/Stop button first then the Beans/Chili button and adjust the cooking time to 15 minutes by pressing the "+" or "-" button.
5. Serve with sour cream or avocado slices if desired.

Nutrition information:

Calories per serving:213; Carbohydrates:47 g; Protein: 6.8g; Fat: 0g; Fiber: 32.1g

White Beans and Sausages

Serves: 8
Cooking Time: 50 minutes

Ingredients

- 4 cups dry white beans, soaked overnight and drained
- 1 jar crushed tomatoes
- 1 tablespoon garlic powder
- 12 ounces kielbasa sausages, sliced
- 1 tablespoon cumin powder

Instructions

1. Place the white beans in the Crock-Pot Express.
2. Stir in the tomatoes, garlic powder, sausages, and cumin powder.
3. Pour 6 cups of water and season with salt and pepper to taste.
4. Close the lid and make sure that the Steam Release Valve is in the sealed position.
5. Press the Start/Stop button first then the Bean/Chili button and adjust the cooking time to 50 minutes by pressing the "+" or "-" button.
6. Do natural pressure release.

Nutrition information:

Calories per serving:241; Carbohydrates: 28.1g; Protein: 16.9g; Fat: 8.3g; Fiber: 7.1g

Easy White Chicken Chili

Serves: 4
Cooking Time: 10

Ingredients

- 6 cups chicken stock
- 2 cans Great Northern beans, rinsed and drained
- 4 cups cooked chicken, shredded
- 2 cups salsa verde
- 2 teaspoons cumin

Instructions

1. Place all ingredients in the Crock-Pot Express.
2. Season with salt and pepper to taste.
3. Give a good stir.
4. Close the lid and make sure that the Steam Release Valve is in the sealed position.
5. Press the Start/Stop button first then the Beans/Chili button and adjust the cooking time to 10 minutes by pressing the "+" or "-" button.
6. Serve with sour cream or avocado slices if desired.

Nutrition information: Calories per serving: 966; Carbohydrates: 103.8g; Protein: 56.2g; Fat: 39.6g; Fiber: 27.6g

Simple 5-Ingredient Chili

Serves: 4
Cooking Time: 15 minutes

Ingredients

- 1-pound ground beef
- 1 can chili beans
- 1 cup diced tomatoes
- 1 teaspoon ground cumin
- ½ cup cilantro, chopped

Instructions

1. Press the Start/Stop button on the Crock-Pot Express.
2. Stir in the beef and sauté for 5 minutes.
3. Add the rest of the ingredients.
4. Pour a cup of water and season with salt and pepper to taste.
5. Press the Stop button and close the lid.
6. Make sure that the Steam Release Valve is in the sealed position.
7. Press the Start/Stop button first then the Beans/Chili button and adjust the cooking time to 10 minutes by pressing the "+" or "-" button.
8. Do natural pressure release.
9. Serve with sour cream or avocado slices if desired.

Nutrition information: Calories per serving: 359; Carbohydrates: 12.4g; Protein: 32.3g; Fat:19.7g; Fiber:3.2g

Slow Cooker Chickpea and Sweet Potato Stew

Serves: 6
Cooking Time: 4 hours

Ingredients

- 2 cans garbanzo or chickpea beans, drained and rinsed
- 1-pound sweet potatoes, peeled and chopped
- 1 teaspoon cumin powder
- 1 teaspoon grated ginger
- 4 cups vegetable broth

Instructions

1. Place all ingredients in the Crock-Pot Express.
2. Season with salt and pepper to taste.
3. Give a good stir.
4. Close the lid and make sure that the Steam Release Valve is in the sealed position.
5. Press the Start/Stop button first then the Slow Cook button and adjust the cooking time to 4 hours by pressing the "+" or "-" button.

Nutrition information:

Calories per serving: 165; Carbohydrates: 32.3g; Protein: 6.3g; Fat: 2.2g; Fiber: 15.2g

Chickpea Tomato Soup with Rosemary

Serves: 4
Cooking Time: 10 minutes

Ingredients

- ½ cup chopped onions
- 2 cans chickpeas, rinsed and drained
- 1 can crushed tomatoes
- 1 fresh rosemary sprig
- 1 cup basil leaves

Instructions

1. Place all ingredients in the Crock-Pot Express.
2. Pour 4 cups of water and season with salt and pepper to taste.
3. Give a good stir.
4. Close the lid and make sure that the Steam Release Valve is in the sealed position.
5. Press the Start/Stop button first then the Bean/Chili button and adjust the cooking time to 10 minutes by pressing the "+" or "-" button.

Nutrition information:

Calories per serving: 115; Carbohydrates: 36g; Protein: 6g; Fat: 2.5g; Fiber: 13g

Crock-Pot Chicken Enchilada Soup

Serves: 5
Cooking Time: 10 minutes

Ingredients

- 2 skinless chicken breasts, cut into chunks
- 1 can black beans, rinsed and drained
- 2 cups tomato sauce
- 2 cups frozen corn kernels
- 1 tsp. cumin

Instructions

1. Place all ingredients in the Crock-Pot Express.
2. Pour 5 cups of water or broth and season with salt and pepper to taste.
3. Give a good stir.
4. Close the lid and make sure that the Steam Release Valve is in the sealed position.
5. Press the Start/Stop button first then the Bean/Chili button and adjust the cooking time to 10 minutes by pressing the "+" or "-" button.
6. Do natural pressure release.
7. Serve with slices of avocado and cilantro.

Nutrition information:

Calories per serving: 368; Carbohydrates: 28g; Protein: 31g; Fat: 6g; Fiber:10.5 g

Bean Turkey Chili

Serves: 6
Cooking Time: 15 minutes

Ingredients

- 1 ½ pounds lean ground turkey breasts
- 1 can tomato sauce
- 1 can chickpeas, rinsed and drained
- 1 can black beans, rinsed and drained
- 1 can red beans, rinsed and drained

Instructions

1. Press the Start/Stop button on the Crock-Pot Express.
2. Stir in the ground turkey and sauté for 5 minutes.
3. Stir in the rest of the ingredients.
4. Pour in a cup of water and season with salt and pepper to taste.
5. Close the lid.
6. Make sure that the Steam Release Valve is in the sealed position.
7. Press the Start/Stop button first then the Beans/Chili button and adjust the cooking time to 10 minutes by pressing the "+" or "-" button.
8. Do natural pressure release.
9. Serve with sour cream or avocado slices if desired.

Nutrition information:

Calories per serving: 231; Carbohydrates: 27.5g; Protein: 19.5g; Fat: 5g; Fiber:9.7 g

Beefy Corn and Black Bean Chili

Serves: 6
Cooking Time: 15 minutes

Ingredients

- 1-pound ground beef
- 1 package frozen corn kernels
- 1 can black bean, rinsed and drained
- 1 can tomato sauce
- 2 teaspoons chili powder

Instructions

1. Press the Start/Stop button on the Crock-Pot Express.
2. Stir in the ground beef and sauté for 5 minutes.
3. Stir in the rest of the ingredients.
4. Pour in two cups of water and season with salt and pepper to taste.
5. Close the lid.
6. Make sure that the Steam Release Valve is in the sealed position.
7. Press the Start/Stop button first then the Beans/Chili button and adjust the cooking time to 15 minutes by pressing the "+" or "-" button.
8. Do natural pressure release.
9. Serve with sour cream or avocado slices if desired.

Nutrition information:

Calories per serving: 348; Carbohydrates: 30.6g; Protein: 27.5g; Fat: Fiber: 7.2g

Sausage and Bean Jambalaya

Serves: 4
Cooking Time: 20 minutes

Ingredients

- 12 ounces kielbasa sausages, chopped
- 1 can red kidney beans
- 2 cups fire-roasted tomatoes
- 1 cup chopped celery stalks
- 2 sweet bell peppers (different colors), chopped

Instructions

1. Place all ingredients in the Crock-Pot Express.
2. Stir in salt and pepper.
3. Pour 1 ½ cups of water.
4. Make sure that the Steam Release Valve is in the sealed position.
5. Press the Start/Stop button first then the Beans/Chili button and cook using the pre-set cooking time.
6. Do natural pressure release.

Nutrition information:

Calories per serving: 409; Carbohydrates: 32g; Protein: 18g; Fat: 24g; Fiber: 10 g

Cowboy Beef

Serves: 6
Cooking Time: 50 minutes

Ingredients

- 2 pounds beef chuck roast
- 1 can chili beans in chili gravy
- 1 can whole kernel corns, drained
- 1 can diced tomatoes
- 1 teaspoon chipotle peppers in adobo sauce

Instructions

1. Place all ingredients in the Crock-Pot Express.
2. Pour 4 cups of water and season with salt and pepper to taste.
3. Give a good stir.
4. Close the lid and make sure that the Steam Release Valve is in the sealed position.
5. Press the Start/Stop button first then the Meat/Stew button and adjust the cooking time to 50 minutes by pressing the "+" or "-" button.
6. Do natural pressure release.

Nutrition information:

Calories per serving: 307; Carbohydrates: 23g; Protein: 37g; Fat: 7g; Fiber:5 g

Overnight Chili

Serves: 6
Cooking Time: 4 hours

Ingredients

- 1-pound ground beef
- 1 onion, chopped
- 1 can chili beans in chili gravy
- 1 can diced tomatoes
- 1 ½ cup vegetable juice

Instructions

1. Turn on the Crock-Pot Express by pressing the Start/Stop button.
2. Press the Sauté button on the Crock-Pot Express.
3. Stir in the ground beef and onions. Sauté for 5 minutes.
4. Stir in the rest of the ingredients.
5. Season with salt and pepper to taste.
6. Close the lid and make sure that the Steam Release Valve is in the sealed position.
7. Press the Slow Cook button and adjust the cooking time to 4 hours by pressing the "+" or "-" button.
8. Do natural pressure release.
9. Serve with sour cream or avocado slices if desired.

Nutrition information:

Calories per serving: 332; Carbohydrates: 31g; Protein:23 g; Fat: 12g; Fiber: 9g

5-Ingredient Black Bean Soup

Serves: 4
Cooking Time: 8 hours

Ingredients

- 2 cans black beans, rinsed and drained
- 1 can salsa
- 1 cup vegetable broth
- 1 teaspoon cumin
- 1 teaspoon paprika

Instructions

1. Place all ingredients in the Crock-Pot Express.
2. Season with salt and pepper to taste and add 2 cups of water.
3. Give a good stir.
4. Close the lid and make sure that the Steam Release Valve is in the sealed position.
5. Turn on the Crock-Pot Express by pressing the Start/Stop button.
6. Press the Slow Cook function and adjust the cooking time to 8 hours by pressing the "+" or "-" button.
7. Do natural pressure release.

Nutrition information:

Calories per serving:337; Carbohydrates:66.1 g; Protein: 22.2g; Fat:1.6 g; Fiber: 16.5g

Slow Cooked Mexican Meatball Stew

Serves: 9
Cooking Time: 8 hours

Ingredients

- 2 12-ounce packages frozen Italian turkey meatballs
- 2 14-ounce cans Mexican-style stewed tomatoes
- 1 can black beans, rinsed and rained
- 1 can chicken broth
- 1 package frozen corn kernels

Instructions

1. Place the meatballs inside the Crock-Pot Express.
2. Pour in the rest of the ingredients.
3. Season with salt and pepper to taste.
4. Close the lid and m make sure that the Steam Release Valve is in the sealed position.
5. Turn on the Crock-Pot Express by pressing the Start/Stop button.
6. Press the Slow Cook function and adjust the cooking time to 8 hours by pressing the "+" or "-" button.
7. Do natural pressure release.

Nutrition information:

Calories per serving: 287; Carbohydrates: 30g; Protein: 16g; Fat: 13g; Fiber: 6g

Chapter 6: Meat/Stew Recipes

Slow Cooked Baby Back Ribs

Serves: 4
Cooking Time: 10 hours

Ingredients

- 3 pounds baby back ribs, trimmed from excess fats
- ½ onion, sliced
- 4 cloves of garlic, minced
- 1 bottle barbecue sauce
- 1 tablespoon ground paprika

Instructions

1. Place all ingredients in the Crock-Pot Express.
2. Pour in 2 cups of water and season with salt and pepper to taste.
3. Close the lid and make sure that the Steam Release Valve is in the sealed position.
4. Turn on the Crock-Pot Express and press the Slow Cook button.
5. Adjust the cooking time to 10 hours by pressing the "+" or "-" button.
6. Do natural pressure release.

Nutrition information:

Calories per serving: 501; Carbohydrates: 32.4g; Protein: 24.3g; Fat: 29.6g; Fiber: 0.5g

Thai Coconut Pork Curry

Serves: 6
Cooking Time: 35 minutes

Ingredients

- 1 ¼ pounds lean pork, cut into cubes
- 3 cloves of garlic, minced
- 1 cup coconut milk
- 1 tablespoon garam masala or curry powder
- 1 thumb-size ginger

Instructions

1. Turn the Crock-Pot Express and press the Sauté button.
2. Stir in the pork and garlic until fragrant.
3. Add the rest of the ingredients.
4. Season with salt and pepper to taste.
5. Close the lid and make sure that the Steam Release Valve is in the sealed position.
6. Press the Meat/Stew button. Cook using the pre-set cooking time.
7. Do natural pressure release.

Nutrition information:

Calories per serving: 244; Carbohydrates: 3.3g; Protein:25.5 g; Fat: 20.1g; Fiber: 1.5g

Mushroom Pork Chops

Serves: 4
Cooking Time: 35 minutes

Ingredients

- 4 pork chops
- 1 onion, chopped
- 3 cloves garlic
- ½ pound fresh mushrooms, sliced
- 1 can condensed cream of mushroom soup

Instructions

1. Turn the Crock-Pot Express and press the Sauté button.
2. Stir in the pork, onion, and garlic until fragrant or until the pork has turned lightly golden.
3. Add the rest of the ingredients.
4. Pour a cup of water and season with salt and pepper to taste.
5. Close the lid and make sure that the Steam Release Valve is in the sealed position.
6. Press the Meat/Stew button. Cook using the pre-set cooking time.
7. Do natural pressure release.

Nutrition information:

Calories per serving: 551; Carbohydrates: 49.5g; Protein: 46.8g; Fat: 20.6g; Fiber: 7.6g

Peach Pork Picante

Serves: 5
Cooking Time: 45 minutes

Ingredients

- 1-pound boneless pork loin, cut into cubes
- 1 package taco seasoning mix
- 1 cup salsa
- 4 tablespoon peach preserves
- 2 tablespoons parsley, chopped

Instructions

1. Turn on the Crock-Pot Express and press the Sauté button.
2. Stir in the pork cubes until lightly golden.
3. Stir in the taco seasoning mix, salsa, and peach preserves.
4. Pour in a cup of water and season with salt and pepper to taste.
5. Close the lid and make sure that the Steam Release Valve is in the sealed position.
6. Press the Meat/Stew button and adjust the cooking time to 45 minutes by pressing the "+" or "-" button.
7. Do natural pressure release.

Nutrition information:

Calories per serving: 145; Carbohydrates: 6.2g; Protein: 21.2g; Fat: 3.8g; Fiber: 1.6g

Quick Swedish Meatballs

Serves: 6
Cooking Time: 40 minutes

Ingredients

- 24 meatballs
- 1 can cream of chicken soup
- ½ cup milk
- ½ teaspoon nutmeg
- ½ cup sour cream

Instructions

1. Place the meatballs in the Crock-Pot Express.
2. In a mixing a bowl, combine the chicken soup, milk, nutmeg, and sour cream. Season with salt and pepper to taste.
3. Pour the sauce over the meatballs.
4. Close the lid and make sure that the Steam Release Valve is set to the sealing position.
5. Turn on the Crock-Pot Express. Press the Meat/Stew button and adjust the cooking time to 40 minutes.
6. Do natural pressure release.

Nutrition information:

Calories per serving: 236; Carbohydrates: 12.2g; Protein: 18.6g; Fat: 12.6g; Fiber: 3.7g

Orange Beef

Serves: 4
Cooking Time: 40 minutes

Ingredients

- 2 boneless beef top loin steaks
- 2 medium oranges, peeled and segmented
- 1 tablespoon dark brown sugar
- 4 tablespoon soy sauce
- 1 ¼ teaspoon cornstarch slurry

Instructions

1. Place the beef, oranges, brown sugar, and soy sauce in the Crock-Pot Express.
2. Pour in 1 cup water and season with salt and pepper to taste.
3. Close the lid and make sure that the Steam Release Valve is set to the sealing position.
4. Turn on the Crock-Pot Express. Press the Meat/Stew button and adjust the cooking time to 40 minutes.
5. Do natural pressure release.
6. Open the lid and press the Sauté button.
7. Stir in the cornstarch slurry which is a mixture of 1-part cornstarch to 2 parts water.
8. Allow to simmer until the sauce thickens.

Nutrition information:

Calories per serving: 283; Carbohydrates: 15.6g; Protein: 24.2g; Fat: 13.5g; Fiber: 2.4g

Pulled Pork

Serves: 6
Cooking Time: 2 hours

Ingredients

- 1 tablespoon olive oil
- 3 cloves of garlic, minced
- 1 onion, chopped
- 2 pounds pork shoulder
- 2 tablespoon dry rub seasoning of your choice

Instructions

1. Turn on the Crock-Pot Express and press the Sauté button.
2. Heat the oil and sauté the garlic and onion until fragrant.
3. Add the pork shoulder and sear all sides.
4. Add the dry rub seasoning and season with salt and pepper to taste.
5. Pour in 2 cups of water.
6. Close the lid and make sure that the Steam Release Valve is in the sealed position.
7. Press the Meat/Stew button and adjust the cooking time to 2 hours by pressing the "+" or "-" button.
8. Do natural pressure release.
9. Once the lid is open, take the pork out and shred using forks.

Nutrition information:

Calories per serving: 443; Carbohydrates: 3.9g; Protein: 38.5g; Fat: 29.6g; Fiber: 0.5g

Slow Cooked Cranberry Pork Chop

Serves: 4
Cooking Time: 8 hours

Ingredients

- 4 boneless pork loin chops
- 1 can chicken broth
- 1 can cranberry sauce
- 8-ounce Catalina dressing
- 1 onion, chopped finely

Instructions

1. Place all ingredients in the Crock-Pot Express.
2. Pour in 1 cup of water and season with salt and pepper to taste.
3. Close the lid and make sure that the Steam Release Valve is in the sealed position.
4. Turn on the Crock-Pot Express and press the Slow Cook button.
5. Adjust the cooking time to 8 hours by pressing the "+" or "-" button.
6. Do natural pressure release.

Nutrition information:

Calories per serving: 422; Carbohydrates: 29.9g; Protein: 50.2g; Fat: 10.3g; Fiber: 1.3g

Easy Slow Cooked Ham

Serves: 10
Cooking Time: 3 hours

Ingredients

- 5 pounds boneless fully cooked ham
- 1 can crushed pineapples, juice reserved
- 1 ½ cups packed brown sugar
- 6 whole cloves
- 1 bay leaf

Instructions

1. Place all ingredients in the Crock-Pot Express.
2. Pour in 1 cup of water and season with salt and pepper to taste.
3. Close the lid and make sure that the Steam Release Valve is in the sealed position.
4. Turn on the Crock-Pot Express and press the Slow Cook button.
5. Adjust the cooking time to 3 hours by pressing the "+" or "-" button.
6. Do natural pressure release.

Nutrition information:

Calories per serving: 441; Carbohydrates: 58.2g; Protein: 40.9g; Fat: 5.5g; Fiber: 0.2g

Slow Cooked Mississippi Roast

Serves: 10
Cooking Time: 10 hours

Ingredients

- 3 pounds chuck roast
- 1-ounce packet dry ranch seasoning mix
- 1-ounce packet dry au jus gravy mix
- 6 tablespoons unsalted butter
- 6 pepperoncini, chopped

Instructions

1. Place all ingredients in the Crock-Pot Express.
2. Pour in 1 cup of water and season with salt and pepper to taste.
3. Close the lid and make sure that the Steam Release Valve is in the sealed position.
4. Turn on the Crock-Pot Express and press the Slow Cook button.
5. Adjust the cooking time to 10 hours by pressing the "+" or "-" button.
6. Do natural pressure release.

Nutrition information:

Calories per serving: 502; Carbohydrates: 2.9g; Protein: 60.9 g; Fat: 26.8g; Fiber: 0.5g

Slow Cooked Honey Mustard Barbecue Pork Ribs

Serves: 6
Cooking Time: 8 hours

Ingredients

- 3 ½ pounds boneless pork country-style ribs
- 18-ounce jar honey mustard
- 1 cup barbecue sauce
- 2 teaspoons garlic powder
- 1 onion, chopped

Instructions

1. Place all ingredients in the Crock-Pot Express.
2. Pour in 1 cup of water and season with salt and pepper to taste.
3. Close the lid and make sure that the Steam Release Valve is in the sealed position.
4. Turn on the Crock-Pot Express and press the Slow Cook button.
5. Adjust the cooking time to 8 hours by pressing the "+" or "-" button.
6. Do natural pressure release.

Nutrition information:

Calories per serving: 322; Carbohydrates: 18g; Protein:29 g; Fat: 112g; Fiber: 1g

Slow Cooked Corned Beef and Cabbages

Serves: 6
Cooking Time: 12 hours

Ingredients

- 3 pounds beef brisket
- 1 onion, chopped
- ½ small cabbage, cut into wedges
- 4 carrots, peeled and cut into 2-inch pieces
- 2 medium potatoes, cut into 2-inch pieces

Instructions

1. Place the beef brisket in the Crock-Pot Express.
2. Pour in 2 cups water and season with salt and pepper to taste
3. Close the lid and make sure that the Steam Release Valve is in the sealed position.
4. Turn on the Crock-Pot Express and press the Slow Cook button.
5. Adjust the cooking time to 10 hours by pressing the "+" or "-" button.
6. Do natural pressure release.
7. Take the beef out and shred using forks.
8. Once the meat is shredded, place back into the Crock-Pot Express.
9. Add the vegetables and season more salt and pepper to taste. Adjust the water if necessary.
10. Close the lid and press the Meat/Stew button and adjust the cooking time to 10 minutes.
11. Do quick pressure release.

Nutrition information:

Calories per serving: 457; Carbohydrates: 16g; Protein:35g; Fat: 27g; Fiber: 3g

Slow Cooked Ancho Beef Stew

Serves: 4
Cooking Time: 8 hours and 10 minutes

Ingredients

- 1-pound boneless beef chuck pot roast
- 1 tablespoon ground ancho chili pepper
- 1 16-ounce jar salsa
- 1 package frozen stew vegetables
- 1 cup whole kernel corn

Instructions

1. Place the chuck roast, ancho chili pepper, and salsa.
2. Pour 3 cups of water and season with salt and pepper to taste.
3. Close the lid and make sure that the Steam Release Valve is set to the sealed position.
4. Turn on the Crock-Pot Express and press the Slow Cook button.
5. Adjust the cooking time to 8 hours.
6. Do the natural pressure release.
7. Once the lid is open, Add the vegetables.
8. Close the lid and press the Meat/ Stew button. Cook for 10 minutes.
9. The serve and enjoy.

Nutrition information:

Calories per serving: 302; Carbohydrates: 28g; Protein: 30g; Fat: 9g; Fiber:5 g

5-Ingredient Stew
6-

Serves: 5
Cooking Time: 30 minutes

Ingredients

- 1 ½ pounds beef stew meat, cubed
- 1 can cream of mushroom soup
- 1 can tomato soup
- 1 envelope dry onion soup mix
- 2 package frozen stew vegetables

Instructions

1. Place all ingredients in the Crock-Pot Express.
2. Pour 2 ½ cups of water and season with salt and pepper to taste.
3. Close the lid and make sure that the Steam Release Valve is set to the sealed position.
4. Turn on the Crock-Pot Express and press the Meat/Stew button.
5. Adjust the cooking time to 30 minutes.
6. Do the natural pressure release.

Nutrition information:

Calories per serving: 472; Carbohydrates: 29.4g; Protein: 52.9g; Fat: 10.4g; Fiber: 5.8g

Slow Cooked Beef Pot Roast

Serves: 6
Cooking Time: 10 hours
Ingredients
- 2 pounds boneless shoulder pot roast
- 14 cups ketchup
- 1 tablespoon Worcestershire sauce
- 1 package mushrooms, sliced
- 3 cups green bell peppers, chopped

Instructions
1. Place all ingredients in the Crock-Pot Express.
2. Pour 2 cups of water and season with salt and pepper to taste.
3. Close the lid and make sure that the Steam Release Valve is set to the sealed position.
4. Turn on the Crock-Pot Express and press the Slow Cook button.
5. Adjust the cooking time to 10 hours.
6. Do the natural pressure release.

Nutrition information:
Calories per serving: 228; Carbohydrates:7.4 g; Protein: 31.3g; Fat: 8g; Fiber:1.1 g

Chapter 7: Rice/Risotto Recipes

Simple Mexican Quinoa

Serves: 4
Cooking Time: 15 minutes

Ingredients

- 1 cup quinoa
- 1 cup corn kernels
- 1 can black beans, rinsed and drained
- 2 cups water
- Salt to taste

Instructions

1. Place all ingredients in the Crock-Pot Express
2. Give a good stir.
3. Close the lid and make sure that the Steam Release Valve is set to the sealed position.
4. Turn on the Crock-Pot Express and press the Multigrain button.
5. Adjust the cooking time to 15 minutes.
6. Do the natural pressure release.

Nutrition information:

Calories per serving: 184; Carbohydrates: 32.8g; Protein: 7.7g; Fat:2.4g; Fiber: 20.3g

Easy Vegetable Fried Rice

Serves: 6
Cooking Time: 10 minutes

Ingredients

- ¼ cup vegetable oil
- 3 eggs, beaten
- 1 bag frozen broccoli, chopped
- 1/3 cup soy sauce
- 4 cups cooked rice

Instructions

1. Turn on the Crock-Pot Express and press the Sauté button.
2. Stir in the eggs for 1 minute or until firm. Set aside.
3. Stir in the broccoli and add the soy sauce.
4. Stir in the rice and eggs.
5. Continue stirring for another 5 minutes.
6. Season with salt and pepper to taste if necessary.

Nutrition information:

Calories per serving: 280; Carbohydrates: 35g; Protein: 8g; Fat:12g; Fiber: 2g

Rice with Parsley, Almonds, And Apricots

Serves: 5
Cooking Time: 15 minutes

Ingredients

- 1 cup basmati rice, rinsed
- 1 teaspoon lemon zest
- 1/23 cup dried apricots, chopped
- 1 cup almonds, toasted
- 2 cups parsley, chopped

Instructions

1. Place the rice and lemon zest in the Crock-Pot Express.
2. Stir in 1 ½ cups water.
3. Close the lid and make sure that the Steam Release Valve is set to the sealed position.
4. Turn on the Crock-Pot Express and press the Rice/Risotto button.
5. Adjust the cooking time to 15 minutes.
6. Do the natural pressure release.
7. Once the lid is open, fluff the rice and stir in the almonds and parsley.

Nutrition information:

Calories per serving: 87; Carbohydrates: 14.2g; Protein: 3.9g; Fat: 5.3 g; Fiber: 5.9g

Mexican Brown Rice

Serves: 6
Cooking Time: 30 minutes

Ingredients

- 1 ½ cups frozen corn kernels
- 1 can black beans, rinsed and drained
- 3 cups brown rice, rinsed
- 1 tablespoon chili powder
- 1 jar of salsa

Instructions

1. Place the rice and lemon zest in the Crock-Pot Express.
2. Stir in 4 cups water and season with salt and pepper to taste.
3. Close the lid and make sure that the Steam Release Valve is set to the sealed position.
4. Turn on the Crock-Pot Express and press the Rice/Risotto button.
5. Adjust the cooking time to 30 minutes.
6. Do the natural pressure release.
7. Serve with chopped cilantro if desired.

Nutrition information:

Calories per serving: 215; Carbohydrates: 41.5g; Protein: 7.8g; Fat: 3g; Fiber: 7.2g

5-Ingredient Fried Rice

Serves: 4
Cooking Time: 10 minutes

Ingredients

- 1 teaspoon coconut oil
- 2 eggs, beaten
- 1 cup frozen vegetables
- 2 cups cooked brown rice
- ¼ cup soy sauce

Instructions

1. Turn on the Crock-Pot Express.
2. Press the Sauté button and heat the oil.
3. Scramble the eggs for 2 minutes or until firm and set aside.
4. Place the vegetables and brown rice in the Crock-Pot Express. Season with soy sauce, salt, and pepper to taste.
5. Continue stirring for 5 minutes.
6. Add the eggs.
7. Serve warm.

Nutrition information:

Calories per serving: 259; Carbohydrates: 32.8g; Protein: 9.4g; Fat: 9.8g; Fiber: 4.1g

One-Pot Fried Rice

Serves: 4
Cooking Time: 40 minutes

Ingredients

- 4 eggs, beaten
- 1-pound sausage, chopped
- 1 ½ cups uncooked brown rice, rinsed
- 3 cups chicken broth
- 1 bag frozen sweet peas

Instructions

1. Turn on the Crock-Pot Express and press the Sauté button.
2. Scramble the eggs until firm for about 2 or 3 minutes. Set aside.
3. Still on the Sauté setting, place the sausages in to the pot and sauté for 5 minutes or until the fat has slightly rendered. Set aside.
4. Place the rice and chicken broth in the Crock-Pot Express.
5. Give a good stir and add the sausages and peas.
6. Close the lid and make sure that the Steam Release Valve is set to the sealed position.
7. Turn on the Crock-Pot Express and press the Rice/Risotto button.
8. Adjust the cooking time to 30 minutes.
9. Do the natural pressure release.
10. Once the lid is open, fluff the rice to combine everything. Stir in the eggs.

Nutrition information:

Calories per serving: 689; Carbohydrates: 66.6g; Protein: 36.6g; Fat: 32.8g; Fiber: 5.6g

5-Ingredient Risotto

Serves: 4
Cooking Time: 15 minutes

Ingredients

- 3 tablespoons butter
- 1 cup Arborio rice
- 3 ½ cups chicken stock
- ½ cup parmesan cheese
- Chopped parsley for garnish

Instructions

1. Turn on the Crock-Pot Express and press the Sauté button.
2. Heat the butter and add the rice. Sauté for 1 minute.
3. Add the chicken stock and stir.
4. Close the lid and make sure that the Steam Release Valve is set to the sealed position.
5. Turn on the Crock-Pot Express and press the Rice/Risotto button.
6. Adjust the cooking time to 10 minutes.
7. Do the natural pressure release.
8. Once the lid is open, press the Sauté button and stir.
9. Add the parmesan cheese until well-combined.
10. Garnish with parsley.

Nutrition information:

Calories per serving: 303; Carbohydrates: 24.8g; Protein:13.2 g; Fat: 20.9g; Fiber: 6.4g

Easy Risotto with Bacon

Serves: 9
Cooking Time: 25 minutes

Ingredients

- 1 tablespoon olive oil
- 1 onion, chopped finely
- 3 cups Arborio rice
- 6 cups vegetable stock
- 6 crispy bacon strips, crumbled

Instructions

1. Turn on the Crock-Pot Express and press the Sauté button.
2. Heat the olive oil and sauté the onion until fragrant.
3. Stir in the Arborio rice and sauté for 1 minute.
4. Pour in the vegetable stock. Season with salt and pepper to taste.
5. Close the lid and make sure that the Steam Release Valve is set to the sealed position.
6. Turn on the Crock-Pot Express and press the Rice/Risotto button.
7. Adjust the cooking time to 15 minutes.
8. Do natural pressure release.
9. Once the lid is open, press the Sauté button and add the bacon.
10. Stir to combine.
11. Allow to simmer until the rice becomes thicker.

Nutrition information:

Calories per serving: 396; Carbohydrates: 64g; Protein: 14g; Fat: 11g; Fiber: 3g

Mushroom, Leek, And Brie Risotto

Serves: 4
Cooking Time: 15 minutes

Ingredients

- 1 ½ cups Arborio rice
- 3 cups vegetable broth
- 1-pound cremini mushrooms, sliced
- 1 leek, chopped
- 8-ounce Brie cheese

Instructions

1. Place all ingredients in the Crock-Pot Express.
2. Stir to combine everything.
3. Close the lid and make sure that the Steam Release Valve is set to the sealed position.
4. Turn on the Crock-Pot Express and press the Rice/Risotto button.
5. Adjust the cooking time to 15 minutes.
6. Do natural pressure release.
7. Stir before serving.

Nutrition information:

Calories per serving: 377; Carbohydrates: 31.3g; Protein: 21.5g; Fat: 25.8g; Fiber: 10.5g

Chicken Fried Rice

Serves: 4
Cooking Time: 15 minutes

Ingredients

- 1 ½ tablespoons olive oil
- 1 ½ to 2 cups cooked chicken, shredded
- 2 cups frozen mixed vegetables
- 2 cup white rice
- 4 ½ tablespoons soy sauce

Instructions

1. Turn the Crock-Pot Express and press the Sauté button.
2. Heat the oil and sauté the chicken, vegetables, and rice.
3. Stir to combine and add the soy sauce. Season with salt and pepper if necessary.
4. Continue stirring for 10 minutes.

Nutrition information:

Calories per serving: 569; Carbohydrates: 96.7g; Protein: 11.9g; Fat: 14.6g; Fiber: 8.3g

Chapter 8: Dessert Recipes

Slow Cooked 3-Ingredient Peach Cobbler

Serves: 8
Cooking Time: 3 hours

Ingredients

- 6 large peaches, peeled and sliced
- 1 package white cake mix
- ½ cup butter

Instructions

1. Place the peaches at the bottom of the Crock-Pot Express.
2. In a mixing a bowl, mix the cake and butter. Cut the butter into the cake until it becomes crumbly.
3. Sprinkle the cake mix over the peaches.
4. Close the lid and make sure that the Steam Release Valve is set to the sealed position.
5. Turn on the Crock-Pot Express and press the Slow Cook button.
6. Adjust the cooking time to 3 hours.
7. Do natural pressure release.
8. Serve with ice cream.

Nutrition information:

Calories per serving: 390; Carbohydrates: 55.8g; Protein:2.7 g; Fat: 17.8g; Fiber: 0.7g

Slow Cooker Fudge

Serves: 10
Cooking Time: 3 hours

Ingredients

- 2 cups milk chocolate chips
- ¼ cup heavy whipping cream
- 1/3 cup honey
- ½ cup white chocolate chips
- Coarse sea salt

Instructions

1. Place the milk chocolate chips, whipping cream, and honey in the Crock-Pot Express.
2. Close the lid and make sure that the Steam Release Valve is set to the sealed position.
3. Turn on the Crock-Pot Express and press the Slow Cook button.
4. Adjust the cooking time to 3 hours.
5. Do natural pressure release.
6. Once the lid is open, stir in the white chocolate chips while still hot. Once melted.
7. Pour the fudge into a baking dish.
8. Sprinkle with coarse salt on top.
9. Place in the fridge before serving.

Nutrition information:

Calories per serving: 126; Carbohydrates: 20.6g; Protein: 2.2g; Fat: 4.4g; Fiber: 0.3g

Crockpot Monkey Bread

Serves: 10
Cooking Time: 2 hours

Ingredients

- ½ cup white sugar
- ½ cup brown sugar
- 1 teaspoon ground cinnamon
- 1 stick butter, melted
- 1 container biscuits

Instructions

1. In a mixing a bowl, combine the white sugar, brown sugar, and cinnamon. Set aside.
2. Cut the biscuits into 6 pieces and dip into melted butter then to the cinnamon-sugar mixture.
3. Place inside the Crock-Pot Express and pour the butter and the remaining ingredients over the biscuits.
4. Close the lid and make sure that the Steam Release Valve is set to the sealed position.
5. Turn on the Crock-Pot Express and press the Slow Cook button.
6. Adjust the cooking time to 2 hours.

Nutrition information:

Calories per serving: 141; Carbohydrates: 14.1g; Protein: 0.9g; Fat: 9.2g; Fiber: 0.4g

Slow Cooked Lemon Blueberry Dump Cake

Serves: 8
Cooking Time: 4 hours

Ingredients

- 1 box Betty Crocker Lemon Cake Mix
- 2 cans blueberry pie filling
- 1 stick butter, melted

Instructions

1. Place the pie filling at the bottom of the Crock-Pot Express and spread out evenly.
2. In a mixing a bowl, mix together the lemon cake mix and butter. Stir until the texture gets crumbly.
3. Sprinkle the crumbly cake batter all over the pie filling.
4. Close the lid and make sure that the Steam Release Valve is set to the sealed position.
5. Turn on the Crock-Pot Express and press the Slow Cook button.
6. Adjust the cooking time to 4 hours.

Nutrition information:

Calories per serving: 449; Carbohydrates: 73.3g; Protein: 4.5g; Fat: 15.7g; Fiber: 2g

Crock-Pot Express Chocolate Bars

Serves: 20
Cooking Time: 3 hours

Ingredients

- 2 cups raw pumpkin seeds or pepitas
- 2 cups crushed pretzels
- 5 cups semi-sweet chocolate chips
- 1 ½ cup butterscotch chips
- ¾ cup creamy peanut butter

Instructions

1. Place the pumpkin seeds at the bottom of the Crock-Pot Express.
2. Add a layer of crushed pretzels, chocolate chips, and butterscotch chips.
3. Place the creamy peanut butter on top.
4. Close the lid and make sure that the Steam Release Valve is set to the sealed position.
5. Turn on the Crock-Pot Express and press the Slow Cook button.
6. Adjust the cooking time to 3 hours.

Nutrition information:

Calories per serving: 286; Carbohydrates: 26.1g; Protein: 7.4g; Fat: 18.5g; Fiber: 14.3g

Chapter 9: Slow Cooker Recipes

Slow and Easy Beef Stew

Serves: 12
Cooking Time: 12 hours

Ingredients

- 2 pounds stewing beef, cut into chunks
- 2 onions, chopped
- 4 carrots, peeled and sliced
- 4 potatoes, peeled and sliced
- 1 can cream of mushroom soup

Instructions

1. Place all ingredients in the Crock-Pot Express.
2. Add 1 cup of water and season with salt and pepper to taste.
3. Close the lid and make sure that the Steam Release Valve is set to the release position.
4. Turn on the Crock-Pot Express and press the Slow Cook button.
5. Adjust the cooking time to 12 hours.

Nutrition information:

Calories per serving: 210; Carbohydrates: 24.6g; Protein: 19.5g; Fat: 4.1g; Fiber: 4.3g

Italian Turkey Crock-Pot Express Soup

Serves: 8
Cooking Time: 6 hours

Ingredients

- 1-pound ground turkey
- 2 cans stewed tomatoes
- 1 packet Italian seasoning mix
- 12 ounces sausages, chopped
- 2 cups chicken broth

Instructions

1. Place all ingredients in the Crock-Pot Express.
2. Season with salt and pepper to taste.
3. Close the lid and make sure that the Steam Release Valve is set to the release position.
4. Turn on the Crock-Pot Express and press the Slow Cook button.
5. Adjust the cooking time to 6 hours.

Nutrition information:

Calories per serving: 296; Carbohydrates: 6.3g; Protein: 32.4g; Fat: 16.4g; Fiber: 2.1g

Crock-Pot Express Spicy Honey Garlic BBQ Meatballs

Serves: 12
Cooking Time: 8 hours

Ingredients

- 2 pounds frozen meatballs
- 2 bottles barbecue sauce
- 1 tablespoon honey
- 2 tablespoons minced garlic
- 1 teaspoon chili powder

Instructions

1. Place the meatballs inside the Crock-Pot Express.
2. In a mixing a bowl, combine the barbecue sauce, honey, garlic, and chili powder. Dilute with a few tablespoons of water and season with salt and pepper to taste.
3. Pour over the meatballs.
4. Close the lid and make sure that the Steam Release Valve is set to the release position.
5. Turn on the Crock-Pot Express and press the Slow Cook button.
6. Adjust the cooking time to 8 hours.

Nutrition information:

Calories per serving: 330; Carbohydrates: 45g; Protein: 15.4g; Fat: 10g; Fiber: 1.4g

One-Pot Tortellini Alfredo

Serves: 4
Cooking Time: 5 hours

Ingredients

- 2 cups cooked rotisserie chicken, shredded
- 2 12-ounce package cheese-filled tortellini
- 1 cup heavy whipping cream
- 5 tablespoons unsalted butter
- 1 cup parmesan cheese

Instructions

1. Place all ingredients in the Crock-Pot Express.
2. Pour a cup of water and season with salt and pepper to taste.
3. Close the lid and make sure that the Steam Release Valve is set to the release position.
4. Turn on the Crock-Pot Express and press the Slow Cook button.
5. Adjust the cooking time to 5 hours.

Nutrition information:

Calories per serving: 906.2; Carbohydrates: 83.5g; Protein:70.7 g; Fat: 99g; Fiber: 3.2g

Vegetable Frittata

Serves: 4
Cooking Time: 4 hours

Ingredients

- 4 large eggs, beaten
- 1 tomato, chopped
- ½ green bell pepper, chopped
- 1 tablespoon chives, chopped
- ½ cup cheddar cheese

Instructions

1. Combine all ingredients in a mixing a bowl. Season with salt and pepper to taste then stir.
2. Pour inside a greased Crock-Pot Express.
3. Close the lid and make sure that the Steam Release Valve is set to the release position.
4. Turn on the Crock-Pot Express and press the Slow Cook button.
5. Adjust the cooking time to 4 hours or until the egg has set.

Nutrition information:

Calories per serving: 187; Carbohydrates: 9.9g; Protein: 12.5g; Fat: 10.9g; Fiber: 0.5g

Crock-Pot Express Chicken Curry

Serves: 7
Cooking Time: 6 hours

Ingredients

- 2 pounds boneless chicken meat
- 1 can full-fat coconut milk
- 1 onion, chopped
- 3 cloves of garlic, minced
- 4 tablespoons curry powder

Instructions

1. Place all ingredients in the Crock-Pot Express.
2. Pour ½ cup of water and season with salt and pepper to taste.
3. Close the lid and make sure that the Steam Release Valve is set to the release position.
4. Turn on the Crock-Pot Express and press the Slow Cook button.
5. Adjust the cooking time to 6 hours.

Nutrition information:

Calories per serving: 175; Carbohydrates: 5.8g; Protein: 30.7g; Fat: 12.1g; Fiber:3g

Easy Sweet and Sour Chicken

Serves: 6
Cooking Time: 6 hours

Ingredients

- 1-pound chicken breasts, diced
- 1 jar chili sauce
- 1 jar apricot or pineapple preserves
- 1 cup chicken broth
- 3 tablespoons lemon juice, freshly squeezed

Instructions

1. Place all ingredients in the Crock-Pot Express.
2. Season with salt and pepper to taste.
3. Close the lid and make sure that the Steam Release Valve is set to the release position.
4. Turn on the Crock-Pot Express and press the Slow Cook button.
5. Adjust the cooking time to 6 hours.

Nutrition information:

Calories per serving: 200; Carbohydrates: 11.3g; Protein: 25.6g; Fat:9.9 g; Fiber: 2.8g

Crock-Pot Express Peach Salsa Chicken

Serves: 4
Cooking Time: 6 hours

Ingredients

- 4 boneless chicken breasts, skin removed
- 1 jar peach preserves
- 1 jar chunky salsa

Instructions

1. Place all ingredients in the Crock-Pot Express.
2. Dilute with ½ cup of water and season with salt and pepper to taste.
3. Close the lid and make sure that the Steam Release Valve is set to the release position.
4. Turn on the Crock-Pot Express and press the Slow Cook button.
5. Adjust the cooking time to 6 hours.

Nutrition information:

Calories per serving: 348; Carbohydrates:17.1g; Protein: 53.3g; Fat: 6.2g; Fiber: 2.8g

Chicken Broccoli Alfredo

Serves: 4
Cooking Time: 6 hours and 5 minutes

Ingredients

- 4 boneless chicken breasts
- 1 ½ jar creamy Alfredo sauce
- 1 teaspoon garlic powder
- 1 cup broccoli florets
- ½ cup parmesan cheese

Instructions

1. Place the chicken breasts in the Crock-Pot Express.
2. Pour over the Alfredo sauce and garlic powder.
3. Season with salt and pepper to taste.
4. Close the lid and make sure that the Steam Release Valve is set to the release position.
5. Turn on the Crock-Pot Express and press the Slow Cook button.
6. Adjust the cooking time to 6 hours.
7. Open the lid and stir in the broccoli and parmesan cheese.
8. Close the lid and turn on the Crock-Pot Express. Press the Meat/Stew button and adjust the cooking time to 5 minutes.

Nutrition information:

Calories per serving: 751; Carbohydrates: 4.6g; Protein: 64.3g; Fat:51.9 g; Fiber: 0.3g

Cranberry Chicken Legs

Serves: 5
Cooking Time: 6 hours

Ingredients

- 10 chicken legs
- 1 can cranberry sauce
- 8 ounces classic Catalina dressing
- 1 teaspoon garlic powder

Instructions

1. Place all ingredients in the Crock-Pot Express.
2. Dilute with ½ cup of water and season with salt and pepper to taste.
3. Close the lid and make sure that the Steam Release Valve is set to the release position.
4. Turn on the Crock-Pot Express and press the Slow Cook button.
5. Adjust the cooking time to 6 hours.

Nutrition information:

Calories per serving: 732; Carbohydrates: 22.3g; Protein: 102.2g; Fat: 23.1g; Fiber: 0.7g

Breakfast Casserole in Crock-Pot Express

Serves: 12
Cooking Time: 4 hours

Ingredients

- 1 roll frozen crescent rolls
- 1 cup pre-cooked sausage, chopped
- 6 eggs, beaten
- 1 tablespoon milk
- 1 cup cheese, shredded

Instructions

1. Place the frozen rolls in the Crock-Pot Express.
2. Sprinkle with the chopped sausages on top.
3. In a mixing a bowl, mix together the eggs and milk. Season with salt and pepper to taste.
4. Pour the egg mixture over the rolls and sausages.
5. Sprinkle with cheese on top.
6. Close the lid and make sure that the Steam Release Valve is set to the release position.
7. Turn on the Crock-Pot Express and press the Slow Cook button.
8. Adjust the cooking time to 4 hours.

Nutrition information:

Calories per serving: 193; Carbohydrates: 2.4g; Protein: 10.9g; Fat: 15.3g; Fiber: 0.1g

Egg, Spinach, and Ham Breakfast Casserole

Serves: 8
Cooking Time: 4 hours

Ingredients

- 6 large eggs, beaten
- ¼ cup milk
- 1 cup ham, sliced
- 1 cup baby spinach
- 1 cup cheese, grated

Instructions

1. In a mixing a bowl, combine the eggs and milk. Season with salt and pepper to taste. Add your favorite herbs, if desired.
2. Place the ham and baby spinach inside the Crock-Pot Express.
3. Pour over the egg mixture.
4. Sprinkle with cheese on top.
5. Close the lid and make sure that the Steam Release Valve is set to the release position.
6. Turn on the Crock-Pot Express and press the Slow Cook button.
7. Adjust the cooking time to 4 hours.

Nutrition information:

Calories per serving: 111; Carbohydrates: 1.1g; Protein: 6.8g; Fat: 8.7g; Fiber: 0.1g

Egg, Bacon, And Hash Brown Casserole

Serves: 8
Cooking Time: 4 hours

Ingredients

- 12 eggs, beaten
- ½ cup milk
- 20 ounces frozen hash browns
- 8 slices of bacon, cooked and crumbled
- ½ cup cheddar cheese, grated

Instructions

1. In a mixing a bowl, combine the eggs and milk. Season with salt and pepper to taste. Set aside.
2. Place the hash browns inside the Crock-Pot Express.
3. Add the bacon bits on top.
4. Pour the egg mixture over the hash browns and bacon.
5. Sprinkle with cheddar cheese on top.
6. Close the lid and make sure that the Steam Release Valve is set to the release position.
7. Turn on the Crock-Pot Express and press the Slow Cook button.
8. Adjust the cooking time to 4 hours.

Nutrition information:

Calories per serving: 465; Carbohydrates: 26.4g; Protein: 23.8g; Fat: 36.5g; Fiber: 2.3g

Slow Cooked Chicken and Gravy

Serves: 6
Cooking Time: 6 hours

Ingredients

- 6 boneless chicken thighs
- 1 packet onion soup mix
- 1 can cream of mushroom soup

Instructions

1. Place all ingredients in the Crock-Pot Express.
2. Season with salt and pepper if necessary.
3. Close the lid and make sure that the Steam Release Valve is set to the release position.
4. Turn on the Crock-Pot Express and press the Slow Cook button.
5. Adjust the cooking time to 6 hours.

Nutrition information:

Calories per serving: 490; Carbohydrates: 25.5g; Protein: 25.8g; Fat: 31.8g; Fiber: 0.5g

Crock-Pot Express Creamy Taco Chicken

Serves: 3
Cooking Time: 6 hours

Ingredients

- 3 boneless chicken breasts
- 1 can crushed tomatoes
- 2 green chilies, crushed
- 1 packet taco seasoning
- 4 ounces cream cheese

Instructions

1. Place all ingredients in the Crock-Pot Express.
2. Pour ¼ cup of water.
3. Season with salt and pepper.
4. Close the lid and make sure that the Steam Release Valve is set to the release position.
5. Turn on the Crock-Pot Express and press the Slow Cook button.
6. Adjust the cooking time to 6 hours.

Nutrition information:

Calories per serving:406; Carbohydrates: 3.8g; Protein: 56.2g; Fat: 17.1g; Fiber: 1.3g

Made in the USA
Columbia, SC
17 January 2021